Baskball Shuffle Offense

By Joel Eaves

SUNVILLAGE
publications

www.sunvillagepublications.com

Basketball Shuffle Offense
By Joel Eaves

Copyright © 2010

www.sunvillagepublications.com

Cover design by www.WebCopyAlchemy.com

Dedication

To my wife, and to the fine young men who have played basketball for me at Auburn.

Acknowledgments

MAJOR RECOGNITION MUST GO TO BRUCE DRAKE for his development of the Shuffle offense. Many new ideas have been employed by teams coached by Bob Polk, Van-derbilt University; Cliff Wells, Tulane University; Bob Spear, Air Force Academy; and "Bubba" Ball of Baker High School in Columbus, Georgia.

At Auburn, I have had invaluable assistance from Athletic Director Jeff Beard; my fine assistant, Bill Lynn; and from every member of our athletic staff. Special credit goes to Mrs. Emily Foster for the stenographic work and to Jorge Haeussler for the art work.

Preface

EVERY IDEA ON OFFENSE WE HAVE EM-
ployed in the five years of running the Shuffle is included in
this book. No details have been withheld in giving the wide
choice of patterns to use.

No claim is made that this is the perfect offense, but it
can be used successfully by teams at any level of basketball.
In our section of the country, high school "B" and varsity
teams are using it, along with several colleges. This is
definite proof that any player can learn and master the
mechanics of playing at different positions as required in
the Shuffle.

The Shuffle offense is of particular value to teams of
average ability and size which must depend on coordinated
team effort to be successful. It also aids each player in developing more skills that will make him a good all-around
performer.

Separate chapters are devoted to free lance play and the
fast break because both fit so well with the Shuffle and add
greatly to the scoring potential. The saturation point has
not been reached, and the possibilities of this offense are
virtually unlimited. Few styles of play give such excellent
opportunities for the lay-up basket, as well as middle-distance shots over a compressed defense.

It is our hope that you will find something of interest
and value as we have done in working with the Shuffle
offense.   JOEL EAVES

Table of Contents

CONTENTS

Chapter I

General Offensive Theory

THE TOUGHEST AND MOST IMPORTANT PART of the coach's job is the never ending succession of important decisions that he must make. Actually every single thing that even remotely affects a basketball squad calls for a decision by the coach, and his success or failure is directly related to his ability to come up with a high percentage of correct answers. To try to insure this high percentage and to aid him in this evaluation, it is vital that the coach settle on certain theories or principles to direct his thinking. Otherwise he is very likely to wander from one idea to another in a state of uncertainty. It is essential to believe and have faith in something and that is the basis for this chapter on offensive theory.

Select an Offensive System

It is generally believed that a coach should decide early on a basic system of play and stick with it. He need not run the identical patterns year after year, but the core of the offense should be retained and variations added to take care of changing situations and different personnel.

We feel that it is impossible to teach a new style of offense and be successful with it the first year. To be very frank, it is doubtful that the coach himself can completely

1

master an offensive plan in that short a time, and certainly the players would experience more difficulty. Efficiency is based on correct repetition until the habit is formed, and only then can a player or a team function properly and as a unit. We compare a basketball team to a delicate watch and the slightest deviation can throw it out of balance.

Modify System to Personnel

As coaches, we are all more or less at the mercy of the personnel on hand. Therefore, it is a must to get the most out of the players we have, and to do that we must learn how to handle them, to recognize their strong points, and then modify the pattern of play so that they can use to best advantage their particular skills. The true test of a coach is not his won-lost record but his ability to get all that his players have to offer. When he gets that, he can hold his head up in front of anyone.

A player can be taught some additional skills, but he cannot be completely changed and made into something he is not. This was brought home to us recently, and it . took too long to realize that we could not completely change a certain boy's style of play. Finally we decided to accept the boy as he was and use what he had to offer. When we did this, the ball club picked up and went on to be a good team. So take what you have, study it, pick out the good things and use them.

Let us be more specific for a moment. If you have the good big boy, use and exploit him. Johnny Dee, formerly of the University of Alabama and now coaching the Denver D. C. Truckers, did this with Jerry Harper and in 1956 won our conference championship. Harper was well supported by some fine athletes, but he carried a big load for the ball club.

In 1958, Coach Adolph Rupp at Kentucky had a fine defensive center and rebounder in Ed Beck, but he was not a great scorer. So Johnny Cox and Vern Hatton were used as the top point men. Beck played his own game and the Wildcats took the conference and national championship.

For the past three years, Georgia Tech under "Whack" Hyder has used two 5' 10" guards, Buddy Blemker and Terry Randall, to spearhead its attack. The offense was well-designed to give these boys the shots they liked and every team in the league respected these two fine players.

One of the very best examples of proper use of team personnel was the coaching job done by "Babe" McCarthy of Mississippi State as he guided his team to the Southeastern Conference title in 1959. Bailey Howell, a tremendous player, was the heart of the offense, and it was impossible to stop him with one man. So he carried the offensive load in State's deliberate attack, which was designed to make it difficult to sink or fall back to double team. In addition, the other fine players on this State team could carry their share of the offense when needed.

So here are just a few examples of good coaching tactics that used particular players to the best advantage by modifying the offense to exploit their unusual talents.

Keep the Offense Simple

Every coach fights that feeling of "we need to add this new option—it will help our offense." This is often dangerous. Like the old saying about pushing yourself away from the table while you are still hungry, it is better to push yourself away from the desk while you still want to add some more offense. A beautiful pattern on paper may be a complete flop when it is tested on the court.

In a pattern offense, we feel that five options with the normal free lance play are sufficient. The first year we used the Shuffle we had only three and stubbornly resisted our inclination to add to the offense. As we continued to use this system, additional options were added, but that was easier to do as we became more familiar with the capabilities of the offense and of the players using it. However, we are very cautious about revisions. When we think we have found something different, we wait for weeks before putting it in. That seems to serve as a cooling off period, during which far more ideas are discarded than added.

Another good point is to be sure that you consider each player and his particular problem in relation to the execution of the new pattern. Try at least mentally to put yourself in his place as the pattern is run and thus determine if he can react easily to the new assignment. It is so very important to avoid any confusion in the player's mind. He must easily understand what he is to do and then be drilled in it until he does not have to think consciously—he just reacts automatically from sheer habit.

Each option in a pattern must have its own signal or tip. Avoid the double signal if at all possible. It is better to have a certain pass as a signal rather than a pass plus a following movement to designate the option. One part of the signal may be seen but the other missed, and with five players involved the chance of error is great. So, again, keep everything as simple as possible.

Move Four or Five Men

Movement is the basic factor in offensive play. It is therefore logical to move as many players as possible. Since many teams rely on strong scoring from the post, they will restrict the movement of the big man, thus leaving four men to maneuver. These four must occupy the defense to the extent that such tactics as double-teaming and sagging are dangerous. If this is not done, the effectiveness of the big man is seriously impaired.

For the team of average size, it is virtually mandatory that all five move in a coordinated attack. The movement of any player must have a purpose and be a threat and a problem to the defense. To accomplish this best, each movement should result in a screen, good rebound position, or a chance to score. Also the movement should be so devised as to be almost continuous. When five players move, someone will be open. It is then simply a matter of *giving the open man the ball at the right time.* Perhaps that is heart of all offensive effort.

Organize the Rebounding

To be successful, a team must get its share of the second and third shots because on many nights the percentage of baskets on first attempts will not be high enough to win. In our league, Kentucky teams traditionally are fine re-bounders, especially on the offensive board. Any time we play them we are forced to figure that they will get 20 more shots than we, most of which will be from the board.

It is very important to organize your rebounding so that your tall men or best rebounders are on the board. This is not easy when tied in with offensive movement and fast break defense. We know it is difficult in our pattern, and to offset the weakness, we give freedom of decision to our better rebounders and take a chance on good reaction to fast break defense.

The majority of missed shots will rebound to the weak side or side of the basket away from the shot. When we were using a single post offense, we wanted to get our center into that weak side position, and with good boys at the post, we had more than average success in this. Now we get our top rebounder into that area against the zone defense better than against the man-to-man.

Permit Free Lance Play

While virtually every high school and college team will have, to some degree, a set style of play, a large percentage of field goals will always result from free lance play. This is as it should be, and if players were sufficiently experienced at this level all of us would be free lancing like the pros.

It is sound belief that any *completely* pattern offense can be defensed, so a reasonable amount of freedom to act on his own must be given to the player. With the increasing use of varied defenses both zone and man-to-man, we are headed for an ever increasing amount of free lance operation.

Be Able to Use the Post Man

At one time we felt that the post had to carry 35 per cent of the offensive burden. Our thinking has changed somewhat, and while it is now directed to better balanced scoring, we still feel that we must be able to use the post when it is to our advantage. We formerly went so far as to have what was called a post offense to insure that we would use the post man enough and to make it easier to get the ball to him. This was in addition to our regular offense and was composed of three definite options. We no longer use this idea as an integral part of the offense, but will certainly have it ready to bring out when the situations call for it.

We have noticed that some teams will not use the post as the ball is first brought into the front court but will invariably take the ball into the corner immediately or after the guards have worked with each other. With no intention to provoke argument, it would seem to be useful to feed the post at any time and from any position. To ignore him consistently at any particular time merely makes the defensive job easier.

Probably the best reason for using the post is that he has a good chance to score any time he gets the ball, and, regardless of what the defense does, the ball cannot be kept away from him for the whole ball game—or even a large part of it. So if a player has the ball within 15 feet or less from the basket, he is a real scoring threat. If he can hook or move quickly for the jump shot, he can get a shot. The only problem then is can he hit the good percentage.

Follow the Lay-Up Threat With the Outside Shot

This may seem to be a peculiar statement and perhaps we are just plain peculiar but we like and employ this theory. Any time a player cuts for the basket, there is an opening in behind him and the defense is always compressed to some extent. With the defense forced back, the outside shot can be taken from closer range and becomes a better percentage shot.

We particularly like to use the screener for this outside shot because his defensive man is often driven back by his concern with the possibility of having to help on the man cutting for the basket. We may or may not then screen for this player as it is not always necessary to do so to help him get the shot. If he gets the ball at the proper time, he does not need the screen. Should the defense consistently switch, we will roll the screener to the basket or screen for him and force one defensive man to switch twice in a short period of time.

Include the Drive, Cut, and Shot Over Possibility

Again some explanation is certainly in order. We have seen many offenses (and had them ourselves) that did not use all of these three basic methods of scoring. We were playing in a holiday tournament a few years ago and chanced to hear a well-known basketball authority say, "There is only one team in this tournament that will take the ball and go for the basket." This jarred our thinking considerably as we knew we were not a strong threat to drive. It is not enough to just tell ball players that the drive is a good play and to go ahead and use it. Instead the opportunity to drive must be a part of the offense and the players told where it is. The shot over should be handled the same way.

As to the cutting part of the theory, we think this is the most neglected part of general offensive play. Maybe the reason is that many players never learn to do anything very worthwhile unless they have the ball. Perhaps the game is too much a shooting contest and players can get the jump shot easily so why give up the ball and then have to get it back to get a shot? Or the real problem could be that skillful feeding is no longer a must to make the ball club, and good passers are not easy to find. Frankly, we lean a little more to the last reason and are becoming more and more conscious of the real need to check a prospect's ability to feed and help another player.

Use the Fast Break

This may infringe on some coaching theories, but we operate with the idea that the fast break basket is too good a thing to pass up. We don't intend to go down the floor slowly every time and face the problem of whipping a defense that is sitting there waiting, ready, and in position to take us on its own terms. We want a better chance than that.

We believe in trying to get the cheap basket, and the fast break presents the best opportunity. It does not have to be a perfectly executed three-lane break. If one man can get ahead of the defense with the ball and score that is enough. A lot of ball games are won by just one field goal and no matter how it comes, it still counts two points.

The increase in zone and pressure defenses in recent years makes it even more important that the fast break be a part of the offense. Not many zones will let you in for the lay-up or close-in shot, so you are forced to rely on outside shooting unless the breaking game is used. Outside shooting percentages will vary greatly on different nights and especially on foreign courts. It is also much more difficult to operate against a good pressing defense if that defense has time to get organized and set for the offensive effort. The fast break that is quickly developed will not give the defense time to really apply the pressure and may well result in the easy basket or at least force that defense to retreat into the front court.

Develop an All-Purpose Offense

In the planning stage of offensive development, initial consideration must be given to combating the more or less basic man-to-man defenses. These would be the sliding man-to-man, the switch, ¾the sink, and the press, and each phase or option should be tested against these four defenses. This test would be more conclusive if it could be done in actual scrimmage and game conditions, and one way to handle this is to let the "B" or freshman team do it. An even better way would be to work on the ideas in spring practice, but colleges are not permitted to engage in spring drills in basketball. We feel that this is a very foolish rule, but our vote would not change it. We also feel that it is bad policy to put in an offensive idea and then have to take it out because it is ineffective. Player reaction to this situation can easily be loss of confidence in the entire offensive plan.

If even one type of man-to-man defense serves to render an offensive pattern useless, that pattern should be eliminated from the offense. For example, we do not like to cross two men and exchange the ball because a good switching defense that plays tight can give you too much trouble. So, as much as possible we try to eliminate the chance to switch on the ball. Otherwise we do not worry about the switch too much and tell our players that since someone is going to be guarding them all the time anyway, they should expect it.

Like the increase in zone defensive play in recent years, we anticipate a similar increase in pressure defenses, especially around mid-court with the purpose of first disrupting the movement and timing of the offensive effort. Various patterns can be devised to attack this defense but that adds to the teaching load on the coach and the learning load on the player. If two clever dribblers and ball handlers are available, let them bring the ball to the offensive starting point on their own initiative and ability. They can do it and it will save the coach adding to the offensive plan. The University of California guards gave a fine example of this theory in Cal's winning effort against West Virginia in the N.C.A.A. finals in 1959.

The trend to varying defenses during the course of play brings about another and very different problem in planning the complete offense. It is not a question of operating against just the different man-to-man defenses, but also against any of innumerable styles of zone defenses. As we see this situation, we as coaches are being forced to balanced formations and free lance play with greater emphasis on creating the one-on-one or two-on-two situations. This will hurt pattern offenses, but even at that, when there is offensive movement governed by a few rules, scoring opportunities will naturally develop. Players can be taught that more screens and openings just naturally develop when players move than can ever be designed in set patterns. The basic problem now is to resist panic when confronted with a defensive change and to realize that when you have the ball you are in good shape unless you do something foolish. You cannot be in great trouble when you have the ball.

Chapter 2

Advantages of the Shuffle

FOR SOME TIME, WE HAD BEEN CONCERNED about our offense and felt that we could do a better job with it. Various ideas had been tested and used, but a feeling of doubt still existed. Serious losses through graduation in 1954 left us with a critical lack of height and experience, and it was apparent that a major decision and revision of our offense must be made. We anticipated and actually had a starting team in the 1955 season that while small by college standards had slightly above average speed plus a great determination to prove its right to play. It did more with its ability than any team we have had in the past ten years. Others had better records, but none gave so much extra to try to win.

The search for offensive ideas began. Films, books, magazine articles, and scout reports were studied extensively. Finally, from a 12-foot piece of film from our 1954 Tulane game (they were using the Shuffle that year) and two articles written by Bruce Drake came the decision to use this offense. We deliberately kept the offense to a minimum number of options that first season of 1955 and have since gradually increased the options.

It takes time to develop an offense, but coaches and players learned much by working with any system. After five years of using this idea, we feel that we know a lot about the Shuffle. Still, there is room for more development, so the search for improvement continues. We do not pretend that this is a cure-all for offensive problems, but it has been good to us. The following are the advantages of the Shuffle.

Continuity of the Pattern

Once the pattern is started, it may be continued virtually without pause or delay until the desired shot is obtained. There is no need to regroup or to have a certain player return to his assigned position. Instead each player moves into a new spot as the pattern is completed and the movement is continued.

A True Team Offense

Every man must be able to feed and to help a teammate with the good pass, the proper screen, and so forth. The offense is not designed for one or two men, hut it is very easy to set up the man who has the weak defensive man on him. As a result, team scoring is usually well balanced and the opponent must plan his defense to work on five men instead of one or two scorers.

This type of play aids greatly in developing good team spirit and morale. A definite effort is made to impress on our players the idea that they are a team and that five men can normally whip two, three, or four, and has an even chance with five. Our 1959 team was the most unselfish group I have ever seen. It made no difference to them who scored the points—they just wanted to get enough to win. As a result, two regulars averaged 13 points a game, another 12 points, another 11 points, and the fifth just under 10 points. We have never had a 20-point-average scorer, and frankly do not care if we never have as long as we can get the good point distribution.

Each Player Plays Every Position

Each player is drilled to operate from all five spots in the offense. While this can be a handicap in early practice with the new players, they learn their jobs much faster than would be expected. They also get a more complete knowledge of the entire team plan and operation, which is very helpful in ways to be explained later.

All Players Move, Handle the Ball, and Get a Chance to Score

In many offensive patterns, two or three players are directly involved while the others are mainly decoys or even less. Those left out will normally do a poor job of what little they have to do. Every player wants to be a part of the offense and to get his chance to do something with the ball. In this offense, he is a definite part of everything that is done. He knows this and will react well to the responsibility. There is little reason to put on the suit unless there is something to do.

Players Must Learn More Basketball

The individual player is forced through necessity to learn more about the game. Basically, he learns five jobs instead of one and must be able to operate efficiently in five positions. We have found that our boys like this and take pride in their knowledge of the game. It is also of great benefit to them if they go into the coaching field,

Preface

EVERY IDEA ON OFFENSE WE HAVE EM-
ployed in the five years of running the Shuffle is included in
this book. No details have been withheld in giving the wide
choice of patterns to use.

No claim is made that this is the perfect offense, but it
can be used successfully by teams at any level of basketball.
In our section of the country, high school "B" and varsity
teams are using it, along with several colleges. This is
definite proof that any player can learn and master the
mechanics of playing at different positions as required in
the Shuffle.

The Shuffle offense is of particular value to teams of
average ability and size which must depend on coordinated
team effort to be successful. It also aids each player in developing more skills that will make him a good all-around
performer.

Separate chapters are devoted to free lance play and the
fast break because both fit so well with the Shuffle and add
greatly to the scoring potential. The saturation point has
not been reached, and the possibilities of this offense are
virtually unlimited. Few styles of play give such excellent
opportunities for the lay-up basket, as well as middle-distance shots over a compressed defense.

It is our hope that you will find something of interest
and value as we have done in working with the Shuffle
offense.   JOEL EAVES

our best players in the game and usually substitute our Number 6 ball player instead of a lower-ranked player. Because normally eight good players are sufficient for game play, we are not forced to use the Number 9 or 10 player simply because he plays a certain position. All players are in competition for playing time, and this has proved to be a healthy situation.

Can Maneuver the Defense

Against any type of man-to-man defense, we can take the defensive personnel into any defensive area we want, thus forcing them often to play in a more or less unfamiliar place. Normally, players either defense outside, inside, or on the post man. Therefore, we figure to have some advantage if we can make a corner man defense outside, a post man play in the corner or outside, and a guard play defense inside or on the post. When you find the defensive man who cannot adjust to the different job, then you are ready and capable of exploiting the weakness. We would have a hard time drilling each of our players in pre-game preparations from every spot in the opposing team's offense. I can recall one particular game where one of our players had eight lay-ups because he had caught a defensive man who was having trouble with a screen from behind.

Offense Can Form Quickly After the Fast Break

Most teams will fast break and therefore are faced with the problem of organizing the offense and getting players into position if a shot is not taken off the break or if a missed shot is rebounded and the ball taken outside. If players work only from definite positions, considerable time may be expended in getting into the proper alignment and starting the offensive pattern. This is easily handled in a minimum of time with the Shuffle as the players simply go to the nearest spot. When the five spots are filled, the offense starts. Though this is by necessity a reaction situation, it is amazing how the players see the entire offensive area and go quickly to the proper spots.

The Big Post Man Is Not Required

Everyone is searching for the big man but not many are fortunate enough to find the one who can make the offense. Thus, the Shuffle is worthy of consideration for any team without an outstanding tall man. Such a team will depend a lot on movement and skillful maneuvers more in keeping with their personnel. We like to have the big man, but only if he can move and handle the ball with the other players. We would not be unhappy to have the 6'6" center who is strong and can run and then supplement his rebounding with average-sized college forwards. The ability of our players to move is a must, and we will sacrifice size if necessary to get that movement.

It is also true that the Shuffle can present a serious defensive problem to the opposing big man if his team is playing man-to-man defense. Regardless of how much defensive switching is employed, he will be eventually forced to defend in an unfamiliar area and to make movements not in keeping with his training, size, and agility. The average size center is given the chance to utilize his normally superior speed and maneuverability, and will often hold his own or better in the scoring battle with his larger opponent. Quite often our pre-game instructions include this statement: "Take the big man outside."

Can Use Different Post Men

One of the most desired characteristics in a coach is the ability to recognize individual skills and to utilize them to the best advantage. Since most players today have worked on post maneuvers, and regardless of size are quite proficient in that area, it is often desirable to rotate the post man. Such rotation is an integral part of the Shuffle, and special options are not always required though they can be devised. An added benefit is the opportunity to force a defensive man to play a post man when he may not have the ability nor the experience to do an adequate job. On occasions we use our guards in such a manner, especially when our boy has an inch or two advantage and has played the post in high school. We feel that the more things we can run, and thus force an opponent to devote practice time against them, the better chance we have for success.

Passing is Simple

Though all players work in each spot, the Shuffle is not a complicated offense. Any boy can learn it and can do his job well in a reasonable length of time. One reason for this is that by design the passes are relatively easy and simple. Every man *must be a feeder,* and to make the job easier, the alignment and court position of each player was established to facilitate the passing game.

Forces All Opponents to Work on Defense

We know from our own experience that many players

rest on defense so that, in their thinking, they can go hard on offense. This is false reasoning. It is impossible to rest defensively against the Shuffle without getting hurt. With every player moving, handling the ball, screening, and a potential scorer, there is constant pressure on the defense and any relaxation by a defensive man makes the offensive job that much easier and the easy basket a definite possibility. We believe completely in keeping all the pressure we can apply on the opposition and even more on offense than on defense. If a team is going to crack, constant pressure will do it. We try to be a threat to score anytime we get the ball no matter how we obtain it.

Players Like the Shuffle

Our players enjoy running this style of attack. They take pride in their ability to play in different spots and to learn the extra tasks required of them. They also realize the importance of helping the other player and can be quite critical of sloppy team play and poor passing. Virtually all of our boys who go into the coaching field will use some features of the offense. This helps us a lot in developing new options and maneuvers.

Shooter Gets the Ball at the Basket

The most desired shot in the game is the lay-up and the most common method in a set offense to get this shot is to dribble the ball to the basket. Now when the driver starts to the goal, every defense man in rock throwing range will try to work on him and he may be running an obstacle course before he can shoot. It is much easier and more desirable simply to get the ball at the basket and that is one important thing the Shuffle tries to do. We feel that this one factor is the most over-looked advantage in the offense: the shooter gets the ball at the basket; he does not have to take the ball with him. If the cutter is free, the defense does not have time to shift its concentration with the pass and pick up the man at the basket.

Ample Opportunity for Free Lance Play

It is the opinion of most observers that the Shuffle is a very strict pattern offense, and it is easy to see why this idea exists. Actually we, at times, have felt that our boys were sticking too closely to the set maneuvers and passing up good middle-distance shots to wait for the lay-up. Much of our concern was dispelled when a thorough charting job on game films revealed that our 1959 team actually had an even balance of field goals scored from the pattern, fast break, and free lance plays. However, we are free to admit that a team can become too cautious and therefore pass up a lot of good percentage shots. There is no way for the ball to get in the basket unless some one shoots.

More and more we stress that at particular times from certain spots definite free lance plays are available. We even diagram these for the player's book to show the chances that come from each of the five spots in the offense. In addition, each player has a variety of moves that he can make from each one of the spots that is a part of the pattern. We realize the danger in a pattern that is too rigid and plan to continue to develop additional free lance ideas.

Another key question is how to run a pattern and also get free lance play. What rules must be devised to hit the happy medium in such a situation? We approach the problem in this manner: encourage the free lance play if based on *good basketball sense*. If a good shot results from the move, the requirement was met. If a player uses poor judgment several times, then he should be corrected by pointing out to him why his decision did not produce anything worthwhile.

It is always wise to permit the player with unusual ability and basketball knowledge to take more things on his own. He will do it anyway unless restricted by his coach. Let the other players know that this boy has your permission to free lance more. We have done this with boys like Rex Frederick, our all-conference forward, and there was no problem with the team's attitude as they knew this boy had the ability to make the plays. Basketball players recognize ability and are rabid supporters of the boys who can really help the ball club.

A Good Offense for Average Team Personnel

We wholeheartedly believe the above statement and, while we have the greatest respect for all our teams, we know that some years we could not match the sheer ability of a lot of our opponents. Actually we take this as a compliment to our boys, who were willing to work extremely hard to offset certain shortcomings in ability and size.

Our belief in this theory is based on the fact that the offensive player gets so much help in this offense. He is not placed in the position of having to make his play in a one-on-one situation and thus forced to try to whip a defensive man who may often be his superior in ability. Instead he receives help from teammates who by clever screening and passing make his job much easier. Actually the ability of his teammates is combined with his in the effort to get the good shot. In this combination, there is certainly added strength and a better possibility of success.

An All-Purpose Offense

The time is rapidly approaching when a team will be forced by changing defenses to have only one type of offense; an offense that can be run with reasonable success against any type of defense. This is a tremendous coaching problem, but we might as well face it because it is here. The pro teams don't have that problem, since their rules limit defensive play to the man-to-man. High school and college teams, however, may face any style and often many of them in one night of play.

It is impossible to have a special offense for each defensive variation. A team can come down the floor, see a 2-1-2 zone, call the defense and go into a planned offense only to find the opponent has shifted to a 1-3-1 zone, or a man-to-man. It is not practical or possible then to stop the offense, call the defensive change, and start another offense because the defense may change again. It is also a major problem just to communicate with five players and be certain that each one knows what the defense is doing. So we are faced with the necessity of developing an all-purpose offense and forced to rely more and more on free lance play and the initiative of the individual. We feel that we can, when in doubt as to the exact defense, use the Shuffle along with good basketball sense and come up with a good percentage play. Any time five men move on offense, some one will be open and it is simply a matter of giving the open man the ball at the right time.

Chapter 3

Player Alignment and Adjustment From Other Formations

THE SHUFFLE IS BASICALLY A PATTERN AND continuity offense from an overload formation and is sometimes referred to as a Double Post offense. Regardless of the name or definition, the positions of the five players on the court are of major importance and behind each position is a very definite reason. If even one man is out of position, the effectiveness of the system can be seriously affected. We actually did not realize this until we took our first film of an actual game. It was a big game to us and winning it brought a holiday tournament championship, but after seeing the game film we wondered how we ever accomplished anything with the offense. We had players all over the place except in the concession stand and cutters wandered around with utter abandon. But somehow we managed to get a few good shots. Right then we saw how much teaching we had *not* done and how important it was to have players in the correct positions.

The positions—or *spots* as we call them—are numbered from one through five, and a player's identity is determined by the spot he occupies on the floor. Some teams use a word system to designate the spots, but we hold to the numbering idea because it is simple and requires fewer words to identify a particular spot. To properly form the offense, it is first necessary to determine or designate which side of the floor is to be overloaded. There are two methods of doing this. We use the rule that the 3 man determines the overload and the offense forms on him (Diagram 1). The players bringing the ball up the floor are told *not* to balance the floor, which means that one man will be closer to the side line than the other. That player becomes the 3 man and we believe it easier for the players to adjust who do not have the ball. Now the 2 man may bring the ball up, but since we don't balance the floor, we can still designate the 3 man because he is closer to the side line. After a fast break effort on which we retain possession and set-up after the break, we then let the ball determine the overload.

The other method of designating the overload is to let the 5 man (Diagram 1) do it by his position on the court and also by holding his hand high above his head. We have no quarrel with this idea; it will work effectively. However, we prefer the first method since we do not have a more or less permanent 5 man and any player may be in any spot. Teams who use the 5 man as the signal normally put the same man in that spot every time down the floor.

Diagrams 1 and 2 illustrate the overload to the left and to the right and the numbered spots. Now let's get into the reasons for the location of these spots.

The 1 man is placed near the foul lane between the foul line and the end line. He will play as deep as the defense will let him and still able to get the ball. This position was selected because 1 is first a feeder and he is in the best possible position to do that job. Secondly, he is a shooter and again this spot offers a very good shot opportunity quite close to the basket.

The 2 man is lined up head on the basket and is always farther away from the basket than the 3 man. We tell him to be at least a step deeper because it will be easier to get the ball to him there. If he is even with 3 or closer to the basket, the defense is more likely to play him tight and give him trouble getting the ball. If the defense steals the pass in that area, they virtually have an automatic basket. Should the defense press the 2 man in his normal position, he has a better chance to cut by for a pass from 3 and a possible lay-up. He is told to be head on the basket to make the pass from 3 shorter and safer and also to make his pass to 1 an easier play. We think this pass is easier because the ball goes to the side of the defensive man and it is not necessary to pass the ball directly through the defender.

The 3 man is told to split the area between the 4 and 5 men and will move up as far as the defense permits. Normally we prefer to get him close because his cut is easier. He is also in a good position to pass to either 4 or 5 as he has the angle pass available that was discussed in the previous paragraph. With 2 trailing him, he can, with normal caution, make the pass to that spot.

We believe that the 3 man must be able to use 4or5to keep the defense fairly honest and with the pass to 2 available, we can start the offense at least three different ways. If we let 3 line up wider, he would have poor position to begin his cutting movement and this maneuver is vital to the offense.

We place the 4 man a step and a half from the side line because we rarely cut to his outside and he faces to the inside. We have him two steps deeper than the 5 man, but other teams who use the Shuffle often set him closer to the base line. He is in better rebounding position there but is possibly not as effective as a scorer. We use him for the drive and jump shot over the 5 man and the higher position seems to make this play more effective.

The 5 man lines up even with the foul line extended and just outside the circle so as to avoid any danger of the three-second violation. While some teams set him at least a step closer to the basket, we prefer to keep him higher because we then have more room to operate in behind him. Also if we want to feed him as we come down the floor, we have less difficulty getting the pass to him.

In starting to teach the Shuffle offense, we tell players first to learn the numbered spots, their exact location, and develop a mental picture of the entire formation. When the player does that, he can understand your comments and instruction and you have less talking to do.

Some coaches, as mentioned earlier, prefer to name the spots. For example, 1 may be called the feeder spot, 2 the top of the circle, 3 the cutter, 4 the corner man, and 5 the post or pivot. This is not a major point for discussion and depends entirely on which method best fits the thinking of the coach.

Next we will use diagrams to illustrate the different alignments that may be used for the Shuffle, plus team movements from the more standard offensive formations into the basic overload of the Shuffle. The offense can be combined with others or extra patterns added with the Shuffle as the base. In it is not intended that all of the following movements be included in one offense. They are presented to provide a choice for the coach who may want to add the Shuffle to his regular offensive system.

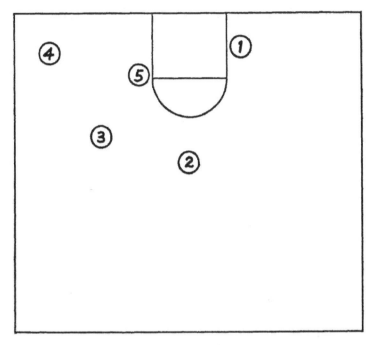

Diagram 1

Overload Left—I man is deep along the foul lane and between the end line and the foul line. 2 is head on the basket and a step behind 3, who is splitting 4 and 5. 4 is close to side line slightly deeper than 5, who is even with the foul line and just outside the circle.

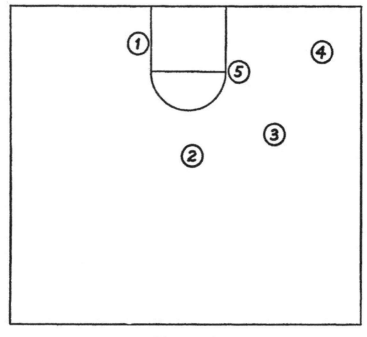

Diagram 2

Overload Right—Side of overload is designated by the 3 man, who is closest outside man to the side line. 5 can also be used to establish the overload.

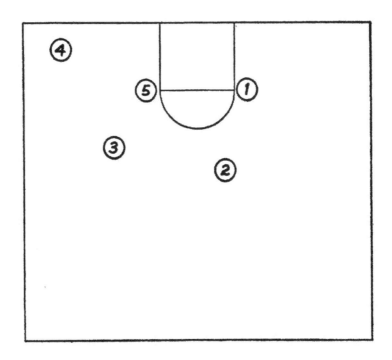

Diagram 3

Variation of Overload—1 man is set high and in similar position to 5. 4 is deep in the corner and 2 is over and slightly inside of 1. This arrangement lends itself well to using two big rebounders as permanent 1 and 5 men and being able to keep them on the board. 5 man should designate the overload by raised hand.

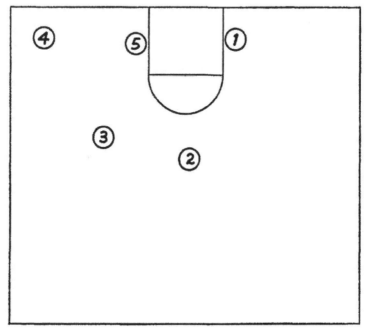

Diagram 4

Variation of Overload—Only significant alteration is the location of the 5 man. Here he is still outside the circle, but is a step below the foul line.

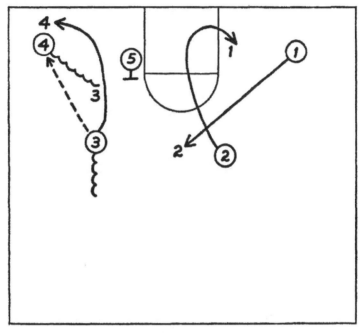

Diagram 5

From Single Post to Overload—3 passes to 4, cuts through and bends out to take 4 spot. 2 cuts for basket and hooks back to take 1 spot. 4 dribbles to 3 spot as 1 takes the 2 spot. 5 steps out to high position at foul line. Shot possibilities on a pass to 3 cutting inside, a pass to 2 on his cut, and 4 driving off 5 for jump shot. These are not drawn in order to leave the diagram easy to interpret.

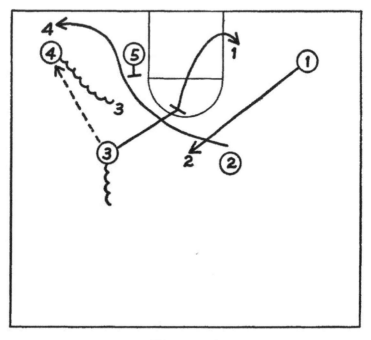

Diagram 6

Single Post to Overload—3 passes to 4 and goes away from the pass to set a moving screen for 2 and then continues to the 1 spot. 2 cuts off 3's screen and if he does not get the pass, he takes the 4 spot. 1 moves to the 2 spot and 4 has the choice of feeding 2 on his cut, driving for shot over 5, or moving to the 3 spot. 5 steps out to get the higher position.

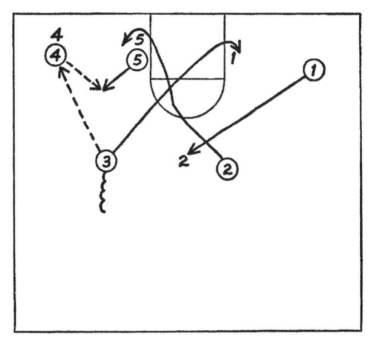

Diagram 7

Single Post to Overload—3 hits 4 and cuts to the 1 spot. 2 cuts behind 3 looking for the pass and will hook back to take the 5 spot if he doesn't get the ball. 5 moves quickly out to the 3 spot as 1 goes to 2. In this diagram, both 5 and 1 move out, away from the basket, and may take their defenders, the opposing big men, to the outside.

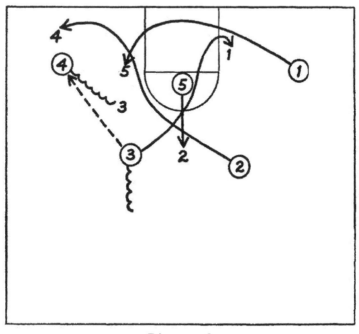

Diagram 8

High Post to Overload—3 passes to 4 and scissors with 2, and then takes the 1 spot. 2 goes to 4 if he does not get the pass. 5 steps out to the 2 spot behind the cutters. 1 cuts across the lane to take the 5 spot. 4 can feed 2, make a drive play to the middle, or dribble to the 3 spot.

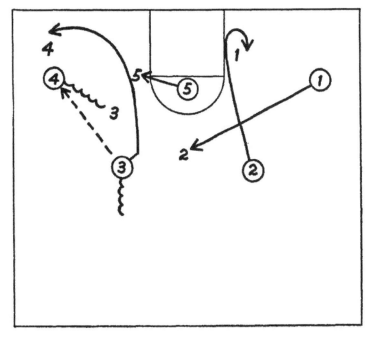

Diagram 9

High Post to Overload—Here is a very simple team movement that we have used effectively. 3 brings the ball up, passes to 4, and cuts through looking for the return pass. He comes out to the 4 spot if he does not get the ball. 4 can feed 3, drive off 5 for jump shot, or dribble to the 3 spot. 2 cuts as the ball goes inside and will be the new 1 man. 1 breaks to the 2 spot and 5 slides to the side the ball is on and takes the regular 5 spot.

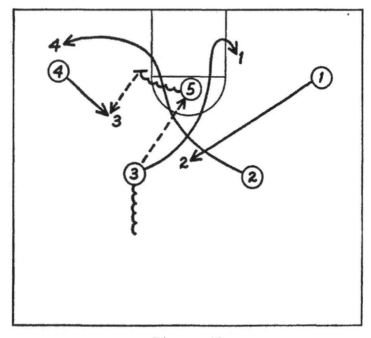

Diagram 10

High Post Split to Overload—This is another pattern that com-
bines well with the Shuffle. 3 feeds 5 and splits with 2. 5 has the
option of feeding either of the cutters, turning to face the basket
to make his own play, or taking the ball out of the circle to the
normal 5 spot in the overload. If he takes it out, 3 will be the 1
man, 2 will go to 4, 1 takes the 2 spot, and 4 moves to 3. When 4
becomes 3, he gets the pass from 5 and the Shuffle is ready to
begin.

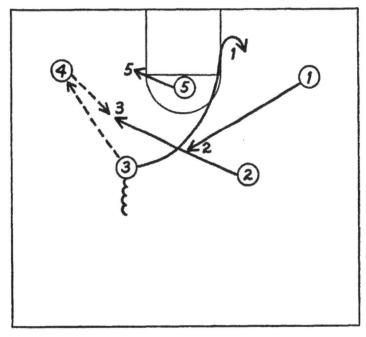

Diagram 11

High Post to Overload—Here is a pattern that presents the opportunity to use the good big man as a scorer from the post while the team moves to the overload. 3 passes to 4 and moves to the 1 spot. This helps clear the strong side for the post man to have more room to work. He will slide toward 4 and if he does not get the ball, he takes the 5 spot. 2 will move to 3 and 1 to 2. When 4 passes back to the new 3 man, the overload is set and the Shuffle ready to operate.

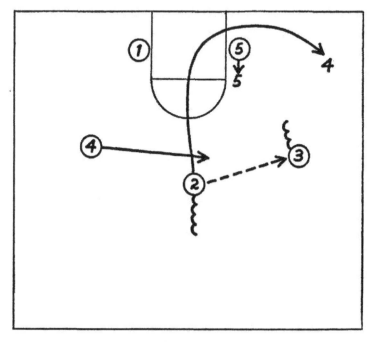

Diagram 12

Close Double Post to Overload—2 brings the ball up and the tip is his pass to 3. 2 cuts through and out to the side of the pass and takes the 4 spot. 3 aids the timing by looking for 5 to feed him if he is open. 4 moves to the 2 spot and 1 holds his position. Since 3 has the ball in good position he can start the offense.

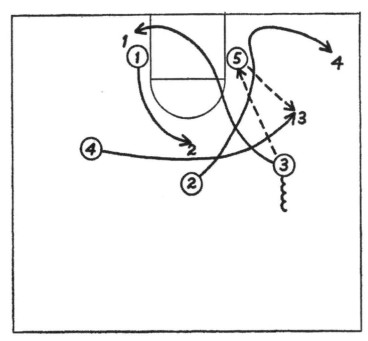

Diagram 13

Close Double Post to Overload—This movement has the advantage of the scoring threat with 2 and 3 splitting on 5. 5 can feed either cutter, make his own play, or pass out to the new 3 man. If they do not get the pass-off, 2 goes to 4 and 3tolasl takes the 2 spot and 4 moves to 3. There is good team movement plus the chance to score.

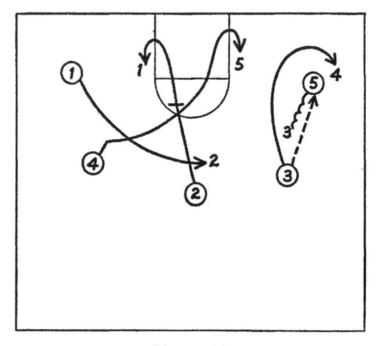

Diagram 14

Wide Double Post to Overload—Here is a pattern which moves all five players, gives the scoring possibility, and finishes in good overload position. 3 passes to 5, moves to screen inside, and then takes the 4 spot. 5 dribbles out to the 3 spot looking on the way to feed 4 cutting off 2's screen. 4 takes the 5 spot if he does not get the pass and 2 screens and goes to the 1 spot. 1 cuts behind 4 and becomes the new 2 man.

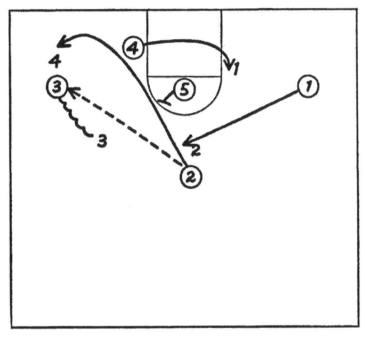

Diagram 15

Tandem Post to Overload—2 passes to 3, cuts either side of 5's screen and turns out to become 4 if he does not get the pass. 4 clears to opposite side of the lane to become the 1 man. 5 screens and slides toward the ball for a possible pass or to set-up in the normal 5 spot. 3 checks 2 and then 5 and if he does not feed either, he dribbles to the 3 spot. 1 moves to take the 2 job.

Chapter 4

The First Option

BEFORE ANY OFFENSE IS STARTED, THE BALL must first be moved into the offensive area. Considerable thought and work should be put into getting the ball into the proper position. Therefore we will begin this chapter with the various ideas that are used to accomplish this phase of the offense.

As mentioned previously, we use the 3 man (the man outside who is closest to the sideline) to designate the overload and any player may be the 3 man. We even have our centers work in that spot if they can do a reasonably good job of it. Our 3 man often brings the ball up, since we use the dribble in preference to passing the ball between two men as they come up the floor. This extra passing presents too many chances for more player mistakes, and mistakes will beat you.

Either 3 or 2 may bring the ball up and we will first consider the variations when 3 is doing this job. We tell him that he is responsible for timing the start of the offense and tell the other players to get down the floor and into position quickly. I can remember Coach Hank Iba saying in a clinic years ago that the ball must be brought down the floor and *taken inside without stopping,* and we have always tried to follow his theory because we have tremendous respect for his basketball knowledge. So, as Diagram 16 illustrates, 3 brings the ball into position and passes without hesitation to 2, 4, or 5. We think that with any offense it is mandatory to be able to start by passing to any of the available receivers. We do not want to pass from 3to1as that is a very dangerous pass across the court, but will use it if available.

As much as possible, explanations are put under diagrams to facilitate reading and study. In Diagram 17, we have 2 moving the ball into position. This is very useful since we often pass from 2 to 1 and with 2 having the ball we eliminate the pass from 3 to 2. Any cross-court pass is vulnerable and when under defensive pressure, 3 may have sufficient difficulty passing to 2 to affect the timing of the offense.

Diagrams 18 through 20 illustrate crossing movements involving 3 and 2 when the former brings the ball up. Notice that 5 and 1 change places. This is not mandatory, but can serve the purpose of moving the defensive personnel and interrupts the defensive thinking of the players involved. This movement also tends to ease the defensive pressure at the 1 spot, making it easier to pass to that player. We do feel that it is more successful if this movement is optional and is initiated by the 5 man as the defense cannot be sure whether the offense will move or not when 3 and 2 cross.

Diagrams 21 and 22 illustrate 2 bringing the ball up and crossing with 3. This is done simply to keep the offense flexible.

Now we are ready to start into the various first options. We have used at one time or other every one of these variations but *do not* have them all in the offensive plan at the same time. We look on this option as a scoring threat but maybe even more as a movement to maneuver the defense and get a defensive man where we want him, plus movement to help hide the basic parts of the Shuffle. We have used a wide variety of first options and continue to experiment on additional ideas keeping in mind always this principle: if the shot is not taken, the players must wind up in the five designated spots of the Shuffle and in good position to keep the continuity of the pattern in operation. This is one option that can be changed with good success during the season. In 1959 we employed four different ideas and were able to execute them after a minimum of practice. The basic tip to set the first option in motion is the pass from 3 to 4.

Diagrams 23 through 27 show the idea we used for the first option when we started to use the offense in 1955. The idea was to change the post man using different players as a post after getting a screen. We even used our 5' 10" captain, Bill Kirkpatrick, in this manner because he had a wonderful variety of shots and could hit a good percentage with any of them. In fact, he could literally drop-kick the ball into the basket, and, being a fine competitor, he took to the idea like he had invented it. We had other boys who had been centers in high school, but were not big enough to combat the normal-sized college post man for an entire game. So we used all of these boys in the 5 spot even if the defense switched and left their big man there to defense our new post man, since the opponent would even then be forced to defend any of several players all with different moves and shots from that area. One other point, the change of 5 and 1 was not rigid and we let 5 initiate it and he could keep the 5 spot if he desired. 3 and 2 were moved to occupy the defensive men and to affect any sink from the front line. Also 4 was at liberty to make his own play at any time he felt he could whip his defensive man.

We have always liked the movement in Diagram 28 and refer to it as *circle,* as well as by the option number. We used this a lot to check the defense, figuring that if the defensive man came with our 1 man along the base line, then the defense was man-to-man. If the opponent ignored 1's move, the defense was a zone.

The *circle* is normally very useful in maneuvering the defensive men into the spots you want them to defend. For example, you can take the opponent's weakest defender to the 4 spot, run the circle once and you have him in the 3 spot where he must defend against a cutter who has the benefit of a good screen. This is normally an unusual defensive job for the player who is accustomed to defensing the corner man or the post man, and there is no opportunity for a switch to help him.

We have used the first option in Diagram 29 more than any other. The 3 man cuts well away from 4 to prevent any switching by the defense and is alert for the pass. This inside cut has proven quite effective because it is a bit unusual to pass to a man on the inside. If the defense wants to switch, 2 cuts straight down the lane and hooks out. If the defense is tight and not switching he screens for 1 to help that player get free for the pass. Diagram 30 shows a variation that has 3 and 2 trading the new spots and also gives 4 a good base line drive opportunity if he takes it quickly after receiving the pass.

The movement in Diagram 31 is quite useful if the defensive man sinks deep off your 4 man as the ball goes away from him. That type of defensive play is very common against the Shuffle, so to offset it you clear that defensive sinker out of the way by cutting 3 to the opposite side and having 4 take the 3 spot. The corner is then completely cleaned out.

Diagram 32 is a well-conceived pattern moving four players and is especially worthwhile if all of your players are equally skillful in playing any place. I would strongly recommend it for a small, fast team with good ball handlers.

We have used the idea shown in Diagram 33, but did not really exploit it to the fullest. Actually, we replaced another first option with this one very late in the season and did not perfect it. We feel that it has good possibilities with an excellent chance to score in close by feeding 5 on the roll-off and the movement also serves to change the overload to the opposite side while the defense is under attack.

Diagram 34 is similar to 29, but is started from a high post formation and moves to the overload while offering scoring chances to 3, 4, and 5. A team that is basically a high post type can mix in the Shuffle by using this pattern.

To maintain defensive balance, we use the rule that the man in the 2 spot or moving to it will balance. He starts to the defensive basket when the ball is shot. The player in the 3 spot or going to it, stops the ball on the outlet pass while everyone else rebounds. This is illustrated in Diagram 25.

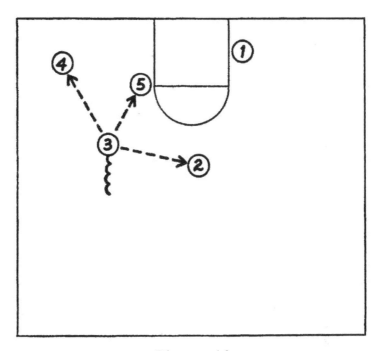

Diagram 16

3 brings the ball up on a line splitting the distance between 4 and 5. From this position, he has good angle passing lanes to 4, 5, and 2.

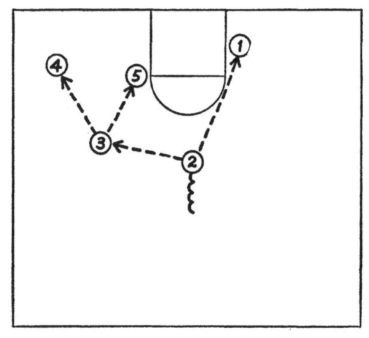

Diagram 17

2 brings the ball straight up the floor and 3 establishes the overload to the left. 2 can pass at an angle to 1 or pass across to 3 who then has the same passing lanes available as in Diagram 16.

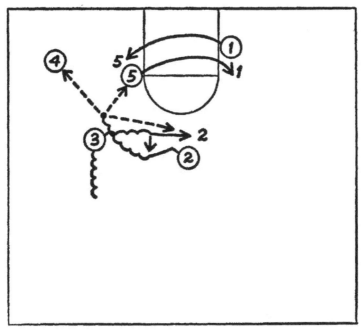

Diagram 18

Here 3 is moving up the floor with the ball and decides to cross and hand off with 2. They then exchange spots and have the ball at 3. 5 and 1 change spots, with 5 starting the movement and 1 crossing behind him.

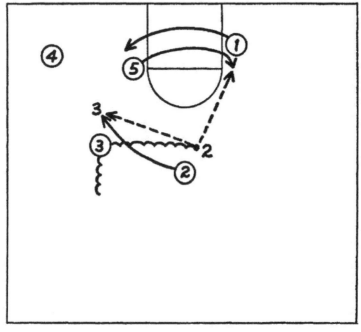

Diagram 19

Again 3 comes up with the ball and crosses with 2 but keeps his dribble taking the 2 spot as 2 goes to 3. 5 and 1 also change places, but remember this should not be mandatory. It is often worthwhile to get the ball to the 2 spot in this manner. It is also surprising how many times 3 will have a good drive opportunity on this, particularly if the defense switches on 5 and 1.

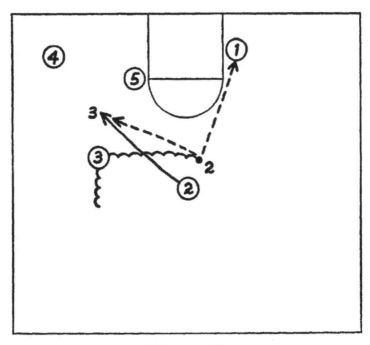

Diagram 20

One of the best crossing movements. 2 and 3 change spots with 2 cutting well in front to deny the defense the chance to switch. The ball is taken easily to the 2 spot as the man in the 3 spot gets very good position to cut if the pass goes to 1. Here 5 and 1 did not change places.

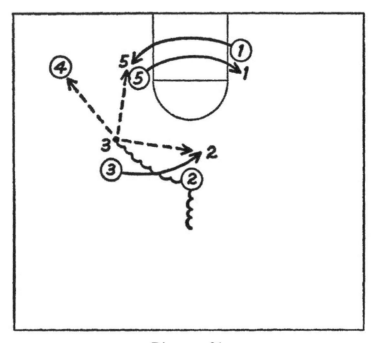

Diagram 21

This time 2 is dribbling the ball up the floor and starts the cross with 3. 2 keeps his dribble and is in position to start the offense by any of three different ways. Again 5 and 1 change spots.

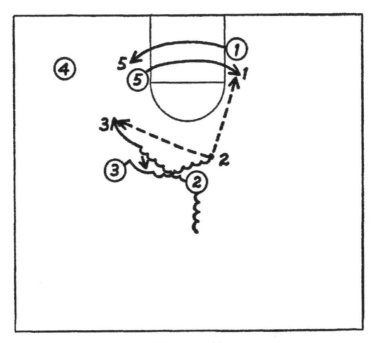

Diagram 22

2 has the dribble and crosses to hand-off to 3. That puts the ball in the 2 spot as 5 and 1 again change sides. This maneuver by 5 and 1 tends to loosen the defense and make it easier to get the ball to the 1 spot.

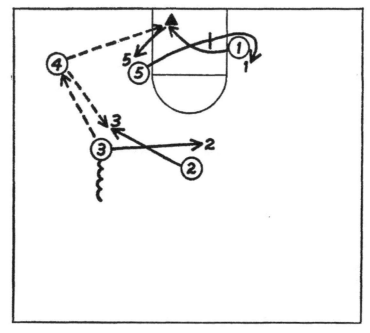

Diagram 23

The tip here is 3 passing to 4. 3 and 2 change spots as 5 screens for 1 and slides off to take the 1 spot. 4 looks to feed 1 cutting over the top of the screen (preferably close to the basket). If he cannot make that pass, he returns the ball to the 3 spot as 1 goes to 5.

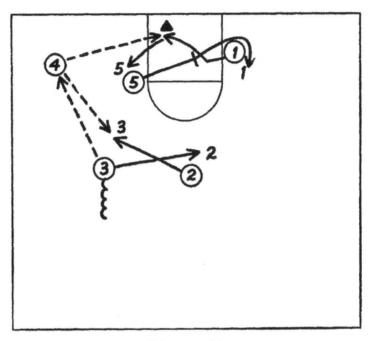

Diagram 24

The variation here from Diagram 23 is that 1 takes the *baseline* off 5's screen. Other players move the same. Quite often 4 can hit 1 before he gets out of the lane giving good position for the close-in shot.

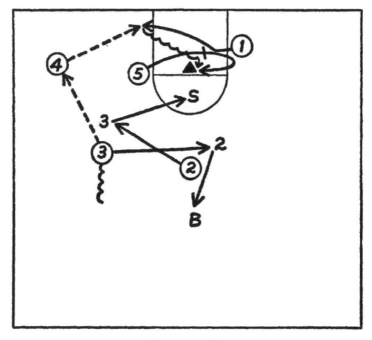

Diagram 25

Here 1 takes the baseline and can't shoot after getting the pass. He then slide dribbles into the lane, which is the tip for 5 to hook back over the top for the shot. Other players make their same moves. Defensive balance illustrated by S meaning stop the ball and *B* meaning to balance.

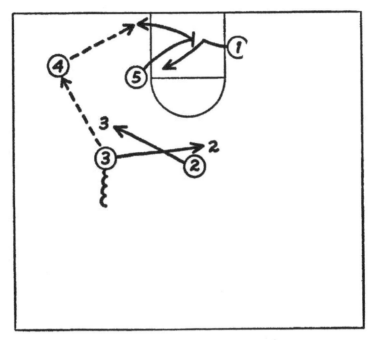

Diagram 26

This maneuver is designed to offset the defense that switches as 5 and 1 cross. Here 5 sets his screen and 1 comes over the top. 5 cuts back close to the board as the switch occurs with the idea of getting the defense behind him and receiving the pass very close to the basket. This should be set-up at a time out after checking the defensive play of the opponents.

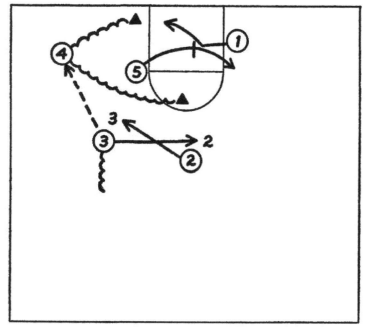

Diagram 27

Here we illustrate the free lance scoring opportunities for 4 on this 1st Option. He can shoot from the side, drive the middle or the base line looking for the good, close jump shot.

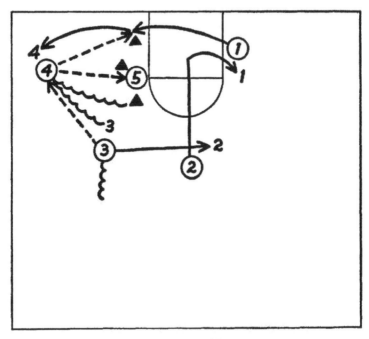

Diagram 28

This first option is often called *circle* and has been used to check the defense and to set-up a certain player by moving him to the 3 spot in a manner that will not let the defense switch. 3 passes to 4 and goes to the 2 spot. 4 looks for 1 cutting the base line, to feed 5, drive off 5 for the shot, or move with the dribble to the 3 spot. 1 takes 4 and 2 goes to 1.

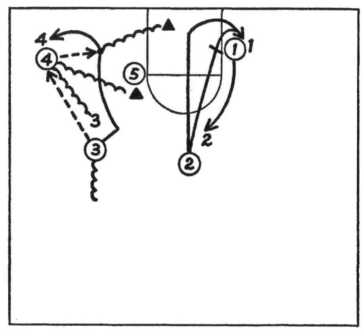

Diagram 29

Another first option we have used a great deal: 3 passes to 4 and cuts inside looking for the return pass or to take the 4 spot. 2 cuts at the same time to screen for 1 if the defense is tight or to cut clean and hook back to the 1 spot if the defense is switching. 4 can feed 3, drive to shoot, or move the ball to the 3 spot.

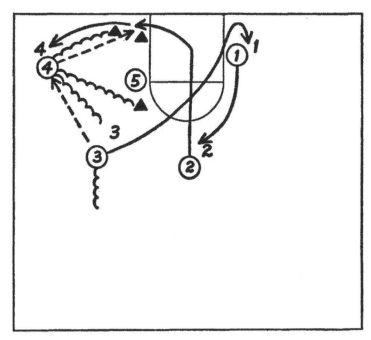

Diagram 30

A variation of the first option: 3 feeds 4 and cuts across to the 1 spot. 2 cuts ahead of 3 and turns out sharply looking for the pass close to the board or to take the 4 spot. 4 has a good drive opportunity to the base line or middle, can pass to 2 or take the ball to the 3 spot. 1 moves out to 2.

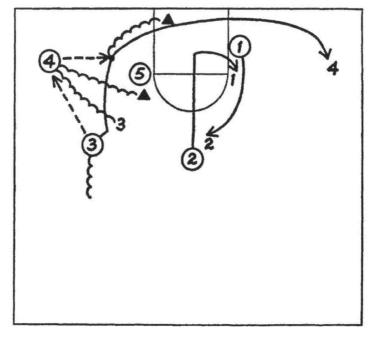

Diagram 31

A good move to eliminate the deep sink off the 4 man: 3 hits 4 and cuts inside looking for the return pass or to continue to the opposite side and takes the job of a 4 man. 4 can feed 3, drive to shoot, or dribble to the 3 spot. 2 and 1 trade places. Pattern is continued as if the overload was still to the left.

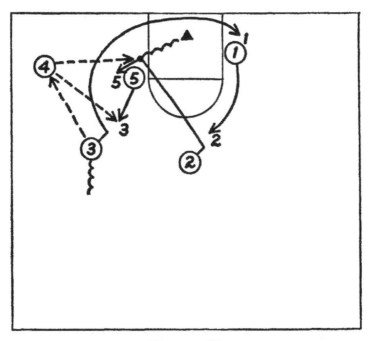

Diagram 32

An excellent first option for a small team: 3 passes to 4 and cuts inside and to the 1 spot. 5 moves to 3 spot behind this cut and 2 cuts behind 5 looking for the pass or to take the 5 spot. 1 moves out to 2. 4 holds his place and passes out to the 3 spot to continue the offense.

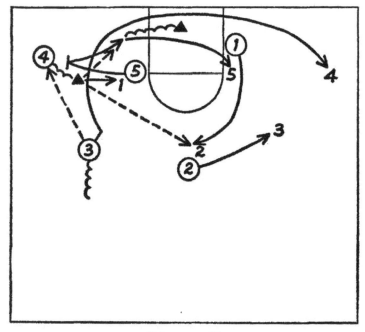

Diagram 33

This option needs a lot of work and timing to be effective. The overload is changed to the right side. 3 hits 4 and clears inside and to the new 4 spot. 5 moves over quickly to set a high screen for 4 and rolls off for the return pass or to take the new 5 spot. 4 looks to give ball to 5, shoot over his screen, or pass to 1 moving to the 2 spot. 4 then takes the new 1 spot and 2 has already moved to 3.

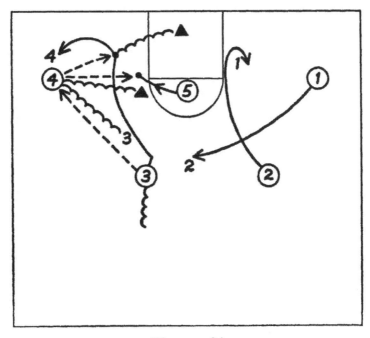

Diagram 34

A first option from a high post and balanced floor: 3 passes to 4
and cuts inside for the return pass or to take the 4 spot. 1 and 2
change spots and 5 slides toward the ball. 4 can feed 3 cutting,
feed 5 at the post, drive the middle, or take the ball to the 3 spot.

Chapter 5

The Second Option

As WE START THIS CHAPTER, LET ME REPEAT again that the several variations shown in this and the preceding chapter are here for the coach to make a choice if he decides to use the Shuffle or to incorporate any part of it into his own offense. It is certainly not feasible to utilize all these maneuvers in the offense.

In using a second option, the first consideration must be how to signal all players that this particular option is to be executed. The simpler signals are used up in designating the first, third, and fifth options, so others must be devised. We are virtually forced now to use a double signal—a certain pass plus the movement of the passer. This can bring problems since every player must see the entire signal, and now he must, in a sense, see *two* signals, which does create a greater margin for error. Frankly, extra caution should be used when installing a second option because confusion brings defeat. In several seasons, we simply eliminated it or never put it in the offense.

The three-man roll involving 2, 3, and 4 is probably the simplest second option to use. It can be signaled by 3 passing to 4 and moving *inside* to *set the stationary screen* as shown in Diagram 35. This fits with a first option that is called by 3 passing to 4 and *cutting clearly through* between 4 and 5 and *not stopping to screen.* Players must see the pass and the complete move by 3 and not just the beginning of that move. The 1 man will have the most difficulty of all in seeing this. The other signal (Diagram 36) of 3 passing to 4 and *going away* or *opposite,* as we call it, is not difficult to see though the 1 man will react a little slower than the other players.

The three-man roll need not go on until some kind of shot is taken and really should be stopped if something worthwhile has not developed after the ball is exchanged three or four times. The roll can be checked by the dribbler simply stopping his dribble at either the 2, 3, or 4 spot and the other two players will be at the remaining two spots or close enough to get to them quickly. Then the next pass can signal and start a different option. As an example, the dribbler stops in the 3 spot, delays for other players to react, and then passes to 2 and starts the third option.

The very popular and widely used *second guard around* series can be easily added to the basic shuffle and called the second option. We have used this idea on occasions, but feel it is wise to have the players with the best speed and ball handling ability in the 2, 3, and 4 spots as much as possible. Since 2 and 3 quarterback the offense as they bring the ball up the floor, they can take care of this problem by using another option if the proper personnel is not in the three spots mentioned above.

Diagrams 37 through 40 show second option variations based on the second guard around principle. Of these, the movement in 39 is the easiest to teach and the most effective. It gives two good opportunities that could not be included in the diagram without congestion. Those are the baseline drive by 4 and the chance to feed 5 after he screens for 2 and then slides back. The best time for 4 to drive is immediately after receiving the pass from 3. It is always easy to feed a player who has just set a screen, so 5 is a good choice and he finds a good drive possibility to the middle through the foul lane.

In Diagram 41, the strong points are the double screen for 1 and the change of the overload from left to right. The 4 man also has good free lance plays when he gets the ball because for a short time his side of the floor is clear and he is one-on-one with his defensive man.

Diagram 42 illustrates the use of a good jump shooter from the 5 spot. For a right-hand shooter, it is best to overload to the offensive right, and to the left for a left-handed shooter. The option is easy to learn, hits fast, and the offense can be continued quickly if 5 does not shoot. All he has to do is dribble back to the 3 spot and make his pass to 3, 4, or 5. Other players have no difficulty in getting into position.

Diagrams 43 and 44 show how to get free lance play from 2 and 3, plus having the other three players in good rebound position. If you have two clever boys who can dribble, feed, and hit good with the jump shot, this is a very worthwhile idea. In addition, the roll-off b y l o r 5 gives the chance to get the lay-up. But remember that the pass to these players is a tough one and requires good ball handlers.

The triple split is becoming more and more popular, and at its worst will deliver a good middle-distance shot. It also follows the theory of following the lay-up threat with the chance to shoot over a compressed defense. Diagram 45 illustrates this type of movement plus the chance for 5 to drive back to the basket. This is a tough drive to defense and 5 has the help of 3 cutting past. This cut tends to freeze the defensive man on 5, plus being a very good fake.

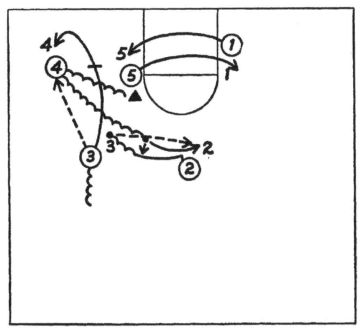

Diagram 35

This second option can be tied in with the first that has the 3 man cutting through clearly between 4 and 5. The tip is 3 coming *close* to 4 and *stopping* to screen, which starts the original 4, 3, and 2 men into a three-man roll or weave. The roll can continue until a shot is taken (for example, 4 drives off 5 for shot) or can be terminated by any man stopping at the 3 spot and passing to the 2 spot. 5 and 1 can change spots as the roll starts.

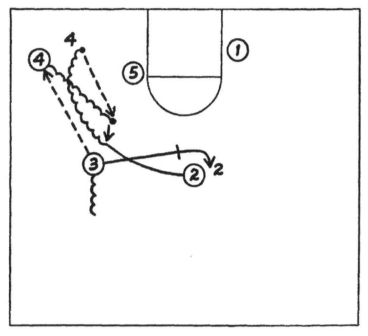

Diagram 36

Another roll or second option variation which is designated by 3 passing to 4 and *going opposite* to the pass to screen for 2. Again 5 and 1 may trade and the roll can be checked as in Diagram 35 by stopping at the 3 spot and passing to 2.

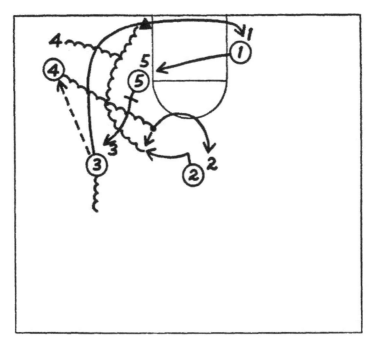

Diagram 37

The very popular *second guard around* series can be incorporated into the Shuffle as a second option. If a team is using a first option that clears the 3 man through and to the other side, this pattern can be used. 4 actually gives the signal after getting 3's pass by a fast dribble to the middle. He passes to 2 who has faked to the opposite side and then takes the 2 spot. 2 drives off 5's screen for a jump shot, continues to the basket or turns out to the 4 spot. 5 then steps out to 3 and 1 moves to 5.

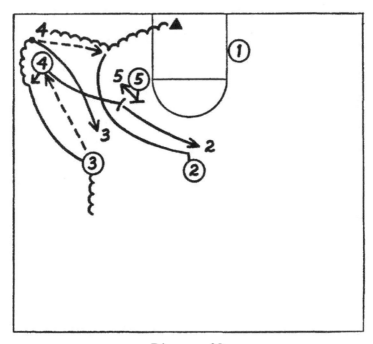

Diagram 38

This second option (another second guard around variation) can be signaled by 3 *bounce passing* to 4 and going outside. 4 hands back to 3 and sets a double screen with 5 on 2's defensive man. 2 cuts off the screen to receive the pass and go to the basket. If he can't get in, he turns out to the 4 spot, and the original 3 man moves back to that same spot. 5 returns to his spot as 4 takes 2. 1 has remained in place, but the pattern could be designated to have him go to 5 and the 5 man go to 1.

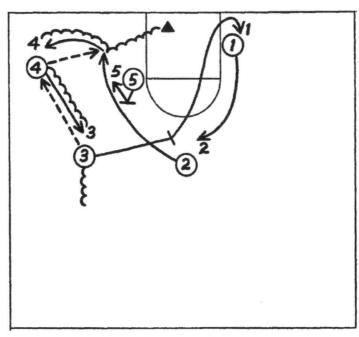

Diagram 39

This option can be signaled by 3 passing to 4 and going opposite to screen for 2 and through to the 1 spot. 4 holds the ball to look for 2 cutting by 3 and 5. If he can or cannot make the pass to 2, he still moves to the 3 spot. 2 will goto4if he does not shoot, and 1 goes to 2. 5 screens and returns to his original position.

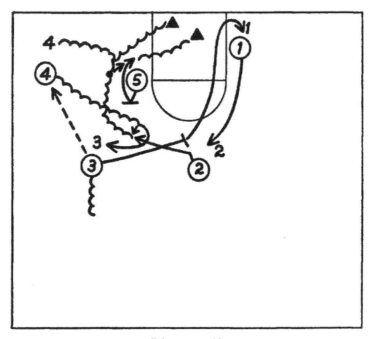

Diagram 40

A variation on Diagram 39 has the 4 man dribbling quickly to the
middle instead of holding the ball on the side. 3 has gone opposite
to screen for 2 and continue to the 1 spot. 2 picks up the second
screen by 5 who can roll for a pass off if the defense switches. If
the shot is not taken, 5 returns to his spot, 4 goes to 3, 3 is at the 1
spot, 2 takes 4, and 1 becomes the 2 man.

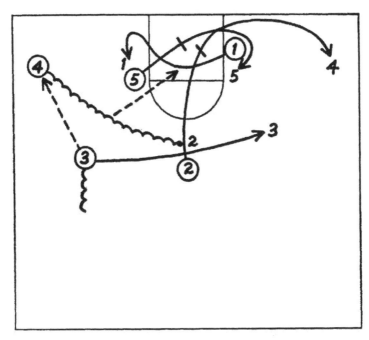

Diagram 41

Here is a double screen and change of the overload side that can be signaled by 3 passing to 4 and going opposite. In this one, 3 goes to the same spot on the other side of the floor. 5 and 2 set the double screen for 1 as 4 dribbles across the middle looking to feed 1 at any opportunity. If 4 cannot make the pass, he continues to the 2 spot, 2 goes to 4, while 1 and 5 take their same numbered spots in a right side over load.

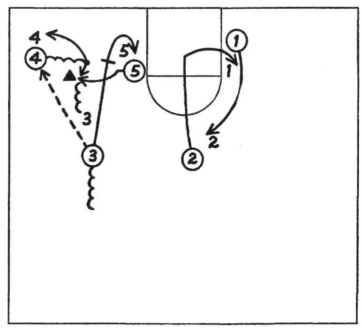

Diagram 42

This second option can be linked with the first by 3 passing to 4 and moving to set a stationary screen for 5. Seeing this screen, 4 dribbles in to form the double screen for 5 to use. If 5 does not shoot, he dribbles out to the 3 spot, 4 returns to 4, 3 goes to 5, and 1 and 2 have changed places. This is effective for the good jump shooter at the 5 spot.

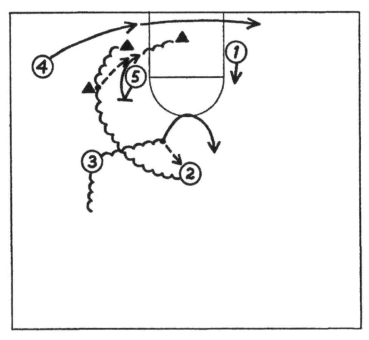

Diagram 43

We have used the cross by 3 and 2 to signal this second option. 3 passes to 2, clears away from him and turns back. 4 moves in beside the lane and clears to the other side as 2 and 5 work a screen and roll play. With two good ball handlers and jump shooters at the 3 and 2 spots, plus good rebounders placed in excellent position in the other spots, this free lance type pattern is quite effective. 2 and 3 balance and stop the ball if the fast break develops, while other players rebound.

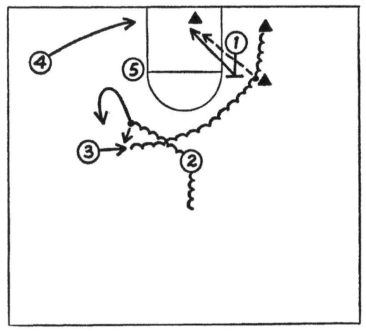

Diagram 44

This is a continuation of the theory advanced in Diagram 43. This time 2 initiates the cross with 3, which is the tip for this option. 2 gives to 3 and clears away to offset the switch. 3 works across to pair up with 1 on a screen and roll. 4 has moved close to the lane for rebound position and 2 turns back as an outlet if 3 needs him.

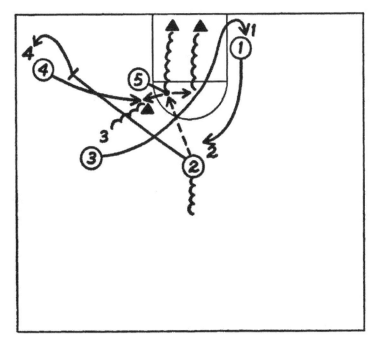

Diagram 45

Here is a triple split that is tipped off by 5 moving into a high post position as 2 brings the ball up. 2 feeds 5 and cuts to make a moving screen for 3 and a stationary screen for 4. 5 can feed 3 cutting, drive back using 3 as a fake, or pass to 4 for the outside shot. If the shot is not taken, 1 has moved to 2, 2 takes 4, 3 goes to 1, 5 returns to his first position, and 4 dribbles out to the 3 spot.

Chapter 6

The Third Option

AT THIS POINT WE COME TO THE BASIC
elements of the Shuffle as it was first devised and what we
now call the third option. This is the bread and butter
play that gives the chance for the lay-up with the middle
distance shot as the follow-up. You will find that it is
actually quite simple and can be added to many of the
standard offenses without great difficulty. Let us first go
over the fundamental plays of the players in each position
as illustrated in Diagrams 46 through 59.

The 1 man is *first of all a feeder* and *then* a shooter *unless*
the defense overplays him and he can quickly make a play
on his own. The 1 man operates along the foul lane similar
to a normal post man except that he will move to the side if
necessary to be open for the pass from 2. He must be taught
to work and to time his move so that he is open at the time
2 can feed him. Upon catching the ball when under
normal defensive pressure, he starts to turn to the *inside,*
pivoting on the inside foot (foot closest to the lane). He
looks first to feed 3 cutting and continues the pivot since
he may find his man open late and in a position directly
behind him. If the pivot is not executed, there is no safe
way to feed the 3 man late—and he is often open then.
Another very important reason for the pivot is that 1 will
be facing the basket at the completion of the turn

and if 3 is covered *but* 1's defensive man is not tight, 1 should shoot the ball. He is within 15 feet of the basket and that is virtually a jump shot free throw. Any decent shooter should hit 50 per cent of these, and we encourage our 1 man to shoot more but *only after* checking 3's chances.

If the defense is tight, 1 will have to protect the ball by catching the pass with his inside leg well advanced, and this tends to restrict or even eliminate the pivot. But do not be disturbed because that type of defensive play is very vulnerable to a quick drive-back play to the outside. And, in addition, few if any teams will have all five men effective in tight defensive position. But if the pressure bothers you simply designate certain players who have the weaker defensive men on them to take the 1 spot as often as they can. Regardless of the defense, it is wise to get your best feeders in this position. The best we have ever had was Henry Hart, an impish 6' 1" jumping jack, who would rather feed than score. He could get the ball to the 3 man despite the defense and, in addition, he could score extremely well from this spot. Another unusual point was that he could draw fouls while working the 1 spot and if his opponent was a key man and scorer, we would put Hart in the 1 spot with instructions to work on his man. The job he could do was amazing and likewise very beneficial.

Now come back to 1 as a feeder. He first checks 3, and if the pass is not safe and he also does not then have a shot, he looks next for 4 and then for 5. I'll be honest in saying that you will not feed the 4 man a great deal. In fact, it is too much to ask the 1 man to do, so let him pass back to 5, who *is* virtually always open. On occasions during the course of a game, you will find that the 4 man is getting open across the lane. At the next time-out, tell the ball club to look for the 4 man and your smart players will get the ball to him.

When a shot is taken, 1 has the job of stopping the ball in the fast break effort and moves into the lane so that he can go to either side. The instant the ball leaves the shooter's hand, all five men are on defense and quick action is an absolute must. Never give up the fast break basket from the board.

Now we will take up the task of the 2 man. He is head on the basket, at least a step deeper than 3, and ready for the pass from him. Upon getting that pass, he must deliver the ball quickly to the 1 man and aims the pass to the *outside* of the receiver. This pass is not difficult as it is angled away from 2's defensive man. After passing, 2 delays *one count* and then moves in to screen for 5. He is told to look for 5's defensive man, find him, and put on a legal stationary screen. He should hold his screen as long as the defensive man is hampered by it and then slide off to be ready to rebound if a shot is taken or to take the new 1 spot. Do not worry about 2's rebounding a close-in shot by 3 because that is asking him to look for a screen and a rebound at the same time, and that is impossible. If 3 misses in that close, you don't deserve a rebound.

You may have decided that 2 is not a threat to score, but that is not quite correct. He will be open many times right at the basket if an opponent is trying to switch on every screen. He also has the chance to score from the rebound and, as you will see in a later chapter, has several free lance opportunities.

The 2 man may also bring the ball up the floor instead of 3, and it is wise to have him do this, The main reason is that the pass from 3to2is eliminated and all you have to do to start the option is for 2 to pass to 1. The tip for the third option is the pass from 3 to 2 when 3 has the ball, but when 2 comes up with the ball the tip is his pass to 1.

Now we take up 3's job. He is a very important man in the offense and you will actually enjoy teaching his plays. The 3 man is ahead of 2 and if he is bringing the ball up, he is running the offense because his pass and resulting move will tip-off the option. In the third option, he passes to 2 but you must tell him more than that—you must insist that he exercise great caution with his pass because an interception means two points for the other team. He can assure this pass by *taking a step* toward 3 and also checking the defensive man in that area. If the defensive man is too tight, 2 should cut as 3 steps (Diagram 59) and look for the pass in the circle. But, for the present, we will assume that 3 gets the pass across to 2.

After his pass, 3 immediately starts to set his defensive man up for the cut off 5's screen. This maneuver permits 1 to get the ball in time to feed. The cut is started under control and 3 must see his defensive man's position. If the defense man is to the *outside,* 3 cuts the *middle* and, if he is to the *inside,* then 3 cuts the *base line* side. Now if the defensive man plays *straight back* and does not favor either side, 3 goes at him and runs him into the screen. Then the cut can be made to *either side.* Some teams will play to the middle regardless of 3's cut, which will either open up the base line cut or the move all the way over the 1 man (Diagram 52). The latter is effective also against the switch, and 3 will have a good, short jump shot with 1 as the screen.

After a shot is taken, 3 is a rebounder and hooks back

to get position. The one exception is when he shoots over 1. Then hc will take the job of stopping the ball and 1 will go to the board. This is a basic rule in our fast break defense plan.

Moving on to the 4 man, he lines up about two steps closer to the baseline than 5 and, as the ball goes from 3 to 2 (or2tol when 2 brings the ball up),he cuts toward the baseline. As he makes the break, he watches for the movement of the 5 man. If 5 screens and then rolls out to the circle, 4 changes direction to cut across the lane for the pass from 1 or to rebound in front of the basket. He cuts *in front of 2,* who is slower because of the screening job for 5.

You will find that a good teaching job must be done on the 4 man. There is a tendency for players in that spot to become spectators, and unless you are thinking and watching for the 4 man, he will not help as much as he can.

The 5 is placed even with the foul line and just outside the circle. He must be alert and expect the ball as it is brought up the floor as well as being ready to screen for 3 when the pass goes to 2 or when 2 passes to 1. When either of these passes is made, 5 steps out one pace to screen on 3's defensive man. This is a stationary screen and 5 must be careful to allow the defense normal room for movement plus remaining still and not moving to make the screen. There is no reason to draw the foul and this point must be stressed to avoid difficulty.

A more detailed explanation of 5's screen is in order. Since 3 is told to take the *opposite* side from where his defensive man is playing, 5 merely steps straight out and does not normally try to screen from either particular side. If, as the game progresses, the defensive men consistently play to one side, then the 5 man should be told to screen on that side. Many teams will try to play through the middle regardless of where 3 cuts. If this happens, instruct the 5 man to screen from the inside. To do this, he steps to place his *inside* foot above the foul line and in the outer part of the circle. He will then be facing *partially toward the side line* and will cause the defensive man covering 3 to use an extra step to avoid the screen. That *one* added step is often enough to free the 3 man on a base line cut.

After screening, 5 delays until 2 is a step away and then rolls out. Now 5 should go only as far away from the basket as necessary to get his shot. His defensive man is often held back by 3's cut, and with 2's screen he can get open in the circle. The diagrams show him farther out but this was done to make the pattern easier to interpret. If the defense plays close, 5 will have to go out to the rim of the circle. Let me stress that he be told to get set quickly and be facing the basket when 1 passes if he uses the set shot from this position. If he likes the jump shot, then getting turned is not as important. When the shot is taken, 5 starts toward the defensive basket as the balance man.

To be successful with the Shuffle, you have to make the third option effective. There are several free lance opportunities that will be discussed in a later chapter and these added to the regular moves in this option are virtually a complete offense. Our 1955 team, dubbed affectionately the "Running Runts" used only *three* options—the first, second, and third.

Now if you will go through the following diagrams and explanations, you will find that this third option is easy to understand and to teach.

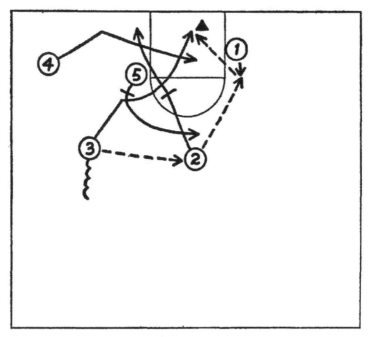

Diagram 46

Three dribbles up with the ball, passes across to 2 and starts his cut. He takes the middle here which he should do when his defensive man is playing to the outside. No. 5 steps out to screen for 3 as 2 passes to 1. Then 2 moves to screen and as 5 starts out, 4 cuts across the lane. No. 1 feeds 3 at the basket.

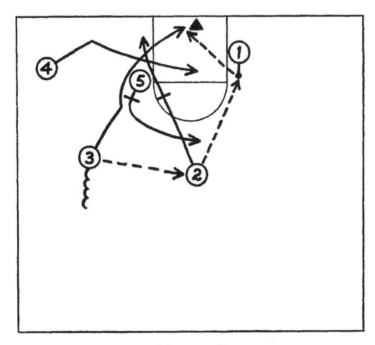

Diagram 47

Here is the base line cut that 3 takes when his opponent is playing to the inside. This point is important—3 should be taught to *slow up* near the basket if he has not received the pass because 1 may have to feed him late. All other players move the same as in Diagram 46.

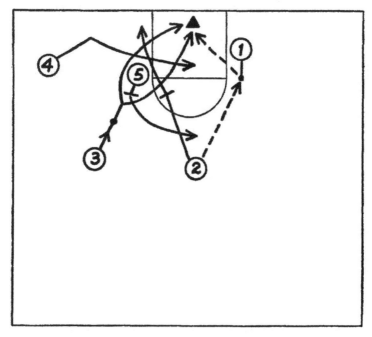

Diagram 48

Two particular things are emphasized here. With 2 bringing the ball up, 3 moves closer to 5 and may even completely stop before he cuts. Since he must wait for 2 to start the pass to 1, he will actually reach the basket a count later because of the reaction time.

Two cuts are shown for 3 to illustrate his choices when his defensive man is straight ahead and will either drop back into the screen or let 3 close too tightly on him. In both cases, 3 has the advantage. Remember that 3 starts under control and uses his fakes to set up his opponent for the screen.

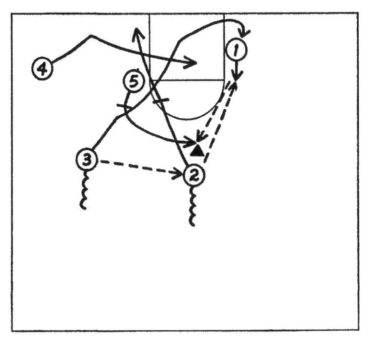

Diagram 49

The wavy lines for both 2 and 3 are merely to illustrate that either one brings the ball up. Here 5 gets the pass and the shot. Let me repeat that 1 looks first for 3, his own play, for 4, and then 5, but he must do this quickly. 5 has the best outside shot in basketball in this situation. It is virtually a long free throw and most boys can hit 50 per cent from that spot.

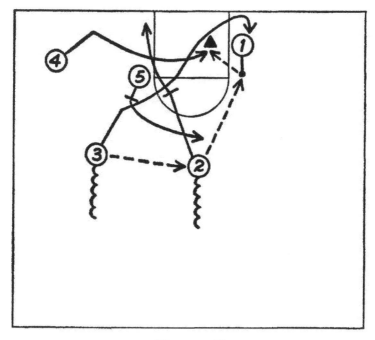

Diagram 50

Here you see 4 getting the pass as he cuts *in front* of 2 and across the lane. This is not as productive as feeding 3 and 5, but it will come in handy many times. It also serves to make 4 a threat to the defense and to put him in good rebound position.

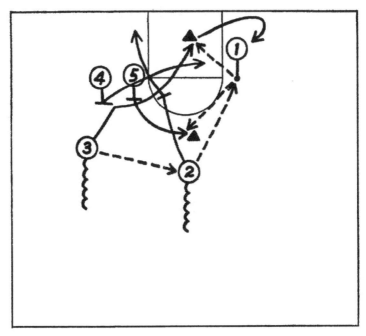

Diagram 51

This is a variation on the usual formation and has been thoroughly tested. It can be used to show the opponent something different and to confuse his defensive thinking. 4 merely lines up next to 5 and that is the *only* change in assignments. 4 steps out to screen with 5 and then cuts behind on his normal path across the lane. 1 is shown feeding 3 or 5 in this diagram. Keep this variation in mind—it can help you.

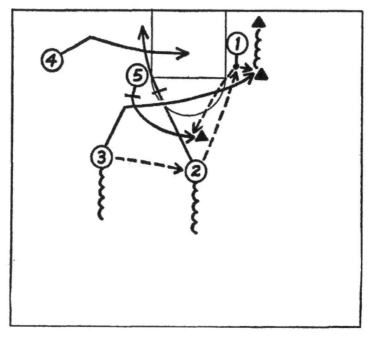

Diagram 52

If 3's defensive man persists in playing through the middle and even leading 3 as he cuts, have 3 go all the way over 1 and look for the jump shot over the screen or a drive toward the baseline. In this case, 3 cuts *ahead of 2* who delays *one count* after passing to 1. All other players have the same normal moves to make. If 3 shoots over 1, then 3 stops the ball and 1 hits the board.

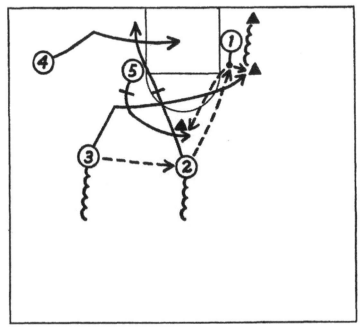

Diagram 53

This is a variation on Diagram 52. Again 3's man is leading him through the middle. 3 decided to cut over 1 *but delays* to let 2 start moving and then cuts behind 2, in effect, getting a double screen. By having 2 delay the one count and putting the responsibility for avoiding contact with each other on the 3 man, you can offer 3 the choice of *two* cuts. 3 must cut on past 1 if he does not get the pass, as that allows 1 then to feed 4 or 5. You will find this a tough move to defense.

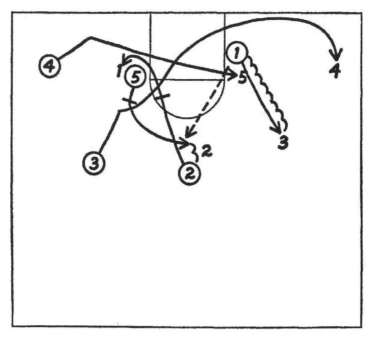

Diagram 54

All passes have been eliminated to avoid a confused diagram. This is to illustrate the *new position* each player takes when the third option is run and a shot is *not taken*. Normally, 1 or 5 will have the ball and by dribbling out (5 is at the 2 spot and merely bounces the ball once or twice) they give other players time to react and get into proper position. We call moving from one spot to another *rotation* and players must memorize the following —*1 goes to 3, 2 goes to 1, 3 goes to 4, 4 goes to 5, and 5 to 2.* The overload has changed from *left* to *right*.

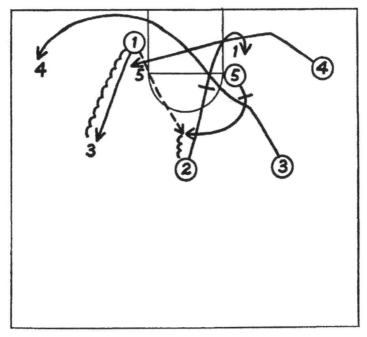

Diagram 55

Here we have the initial overload to the *right,* the players rotate and the finish is an overload on the *left side.* You should draw this from *both sides* for your players as it is much easier for them to understand. Here is one big advantage of the Shuffle—the ability to run an option and be able to quickly repeat it or run a different one.

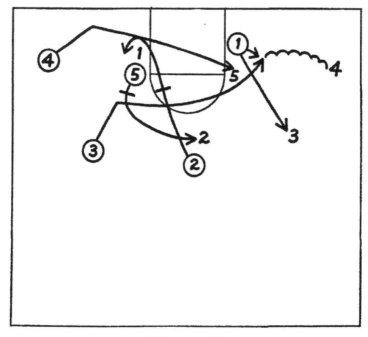

Diagram 56

It would be natural to wonder how the rotation works when 3 cuts over 1, but actually there is no major change. Here 1 passes to 3 who cannot shoot and merely dribbles to the 4 spot—his normal rotation. 1 moves out to 3, 2 takes the 1 spot, 4 goes to 5, and 5 to 2.

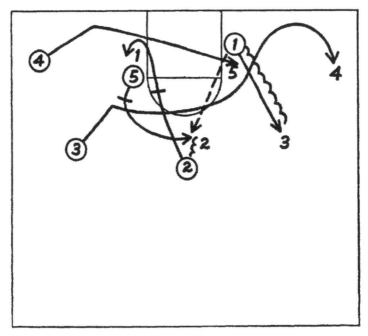

Diagram 57

Now the rotation when 3 cuts over 1 but does not get the pass: 3 continues his cut and when 1 or 5 dribble out, 3 goes to 4, 1 to 3, 2 t o 1 , 4 to 5, and 5 to 2. The rotation is repeated here to help you learn it, and you will find it is not too difficult.

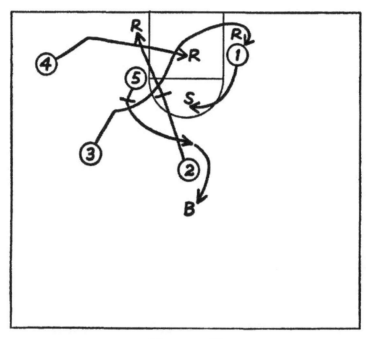

Diagram 58

This diagram illustrates what is called *defensive balance,* referring to the team plan to defense the fast break effort by the opponent. 2, 3, and 4 are rebounders. 1 has the job of *stopping the ball,* and 5 is the *balance man* and defends the opposing basket. 1 is actually a half rebounder and can even be given the full job against a team that does not fast break.

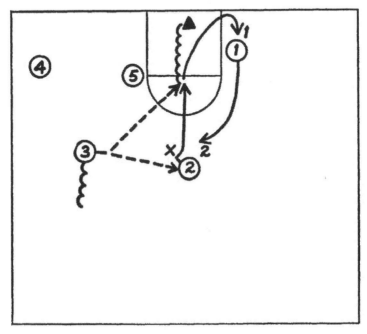

Diagram 59

You will find that teams will often press the 2 man to stop the pass from 3. To offset this, have 2 cut as 3 steps toward him. If he does not get the pass, 2 takes the 1 spot and 1 moves to 2. This will make it easier to get the ball to the 2 spot, as few defensive men can play tight *moving away* from the basket. It is also difficult to switch and stay tight because of 2's threat to score. This maneuver is called *change*.

Chapter 7

The Fourth Option

THIS IS PROBABLY THE BEST VARIATION OR addition to the original Shuffle offense that we know, and in all fairness must give most of the credit to Bob Polk, the very fine coach of the Vanderbilt Commodores. Oddly enough, Bob started using parts of the Shuffle at the same time we did, but neither of us knew the other was changing offenses until the 1955 season began.

To our way of thinking, *jour* things brought about this fourth option. First, the 4 man was not doing enough in the offense, and it is foolish to operate with only four and a half men. Every man must be a scorer, and you must arrange your offense to give them all a chance to shoot from the pattern. If you will now check Diagram 60, you will see that 4 is given help by 2's screen, and you will also have a better background for the rest of the material in this chapter.

The defensive play by opposing teams was the second factor. Many of them had the defensive man on 4 sink very fast to the inside when 3 passed to 2. From that position, the sinker could partially jam the basket area and often deliberately moved in front of 3 on his base line cut. Since the 4 man was always cutting close across the lane, he actually moved into the defensive range of the sinker. This defensive theory was very sound, and it became obvious that a revision had to be made. The conclusion was to vary 4's cut and assist him to score (Diagram 62). The fourth option was the result.

The third factor was the desire to get the best rebounder on the board, especially if he was a big boy who did not operate too well in the other four spots. With the fourth option you can keep such a player at the 5 spot because in the rotation he still is a 5 man and 4 is the player who goes to 2. You can also use the 5 man as a close-in scoring threat (Diagram 61).

The fourth and last reason was to help offset the defensive switch as 3 cut by 5's screen. You need not be overly concerned about the switch because it is extremely difficult to keep switching perfectly when all players are forced to change defensive assignments quickly and often as they must do against the Shuffle. You will find that suddenly a player close to the basket has no one guarding him.

Let us now discuss 5's screen on this option when the defense is switching. He would like to get between the man who switches to him and the basket, and two types of screen can be used. First, 5 can step out facing the man to be screened, then pivot on the inside foot to face the ball and keep the defense behind him when the switch occurs. Remember that 1 has the ball at this time. The second idea on this screen is for 5 to turn, as he steps out, and *face the basket.* He will then actually screen with his back and immediately has the *inside* on the defensive man when the switch is executed.

You may recall in Chapter 6 when we discussed the play of the 4 man on the third option the point was made that 4 watched to see what 5 did after he screened. On the third option, 5 *rolls out,* and that is 4's tip to cut close across the foul lane. Now in the fourth option, 5 *slides back* toward the basket and that movement tells 4 to come out over 2's screen. So 5 actually calls the fourth option and 4 reacts to 5's move. The other three players are not handicapped by this and 4 is not affected at all. The 2 man is moving in to screen, and when he sees 5 slide back he simply screens for 4. This is not a problem because 4 cuts a similar path as 5 on the third option and leads his defensive man to the screen. The 1 man has the toughest job, but when he does not feed 3 cutting, he is looking to the inside and can find 5 without difficulty. If he does not pass to 5, he knows from practice and drill that 4 is coming out and over 2's screen and will be open at the circle.

Diagrams 60 through 62 show the basic movements and shot opportunities in the fourth option. In Diagram 60, 3 gets the shot as he often does in the third option. Diagram 61 shows 5 sliding back after his screen and getting the pass from 1. It is best to teach 5 just to look for the open spot and not always to make a cut straight to the basket. The main consideration is for 5 just to get open so 1 can give him the ball. Diagram 62 illustrates the way 4 gets his shot, and I want to point out that 4 can usually get the pass *in the circle* and not have to go all the way out to the top. Remember his defensive man will always sink toward the middle and will have a relatively long way to go to recover position.

In Diagram 63, the normal shot opportunities for 4 and 5 are again shown plus *the cut by 3 over the 1 man.* This cut by 3 is not hindered by the fact that you have a fourth option, and 3 always has the choice of *three different cuts.*

Diagram 64 shows the *rotation.* Notice that the *only changes* from the third option involve the 4 and 5 man.

These two simply switch the spots they take in the rotation, and since 5 really calls the option and 4 always reacts from his move, you will not have a coaching problem here. Actually, the rotation is slightly faster than in the third option.

In the next illustration, Diagram 65, the fourth option is shown in slightly revised form. The 5 man and 2 form a double screen for 4, then 5 slides over 2 toward the basket. We used this idea first, but changed to the other version several years ago. Either is effective and you can take your choice.

Diagrams 66 and 68 show another version of the fourth option when 5 is basically a screen and rebounder and not a shooter. In *66,* he turns toward 4 and screens for him, and in 68, he screens for 1 to drive. Note that 2 does not go in to screen—he goes toward 1, but not close to him. One big advantage of this theory is that you can take *two* big men and use them in the 1 and 5 spots as feeders, screeners, and rebounders. The other three players rotate to the 2, 3, and 4 spots. This theory is sound and worthy of intense considerations when using this offense.

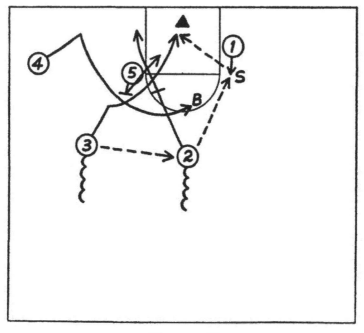

Diagram 60

3 or 2 brings the ball up and 3 cuts off 5's screen and through the middle to get the shot in this instance. 3's play is the same in the third and the fourth options. 5 screens and slides back to get open or to rebound. 4 sees 5 turn back—that is his tip to cut over 2's screen looking for the shot at the circle. 2 passes to 1 and moves in to screen after the one count delay. He sees 5 slide back and then knows to look for 4's defensive man. The S means that 1 stops the ball and 4 balances if the opposing team tries to fast break.

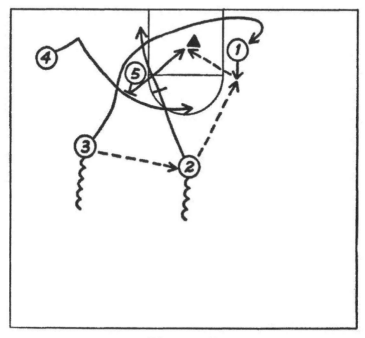

Diagram 61

In this case, 5 gets the pass and the shot. Remember he will do this a lot against a switching defense in the effort to get the defensive man (who has switched from 3) behind him or on the side away from the ball. He may screen face-on and pivot on the inside foot, or screen with his back as he faces the basket.

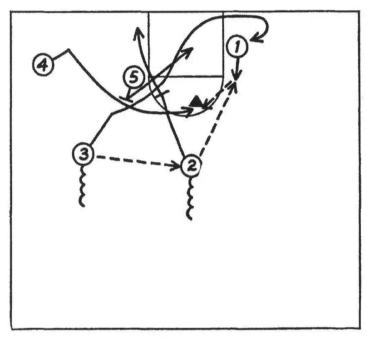

Diagram 62

Here it is 4 who gets the pass and the shot. He can often get a closer shot than 5 does on the third option because his defensive man often sinks too far and 2 also sets the screen closer to the basket. Jimmy Lee, a fine jump shooter, hit three shots in succession from the 4 spot on this option to win a most critical game for us in 1959.

Since 5 is often bumped when screening for 3, it is a good rule to have him run the fourth option when he makes a good screen and contact occurs. If he runs the third, he will be late rolling out and thus confuse the 4 man.

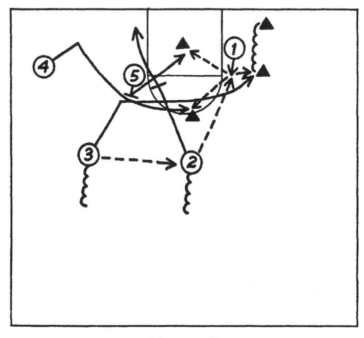

Diagram 63

This is drawn to illustrate the choice 3 may take of cutting all the way over the 1 man. As in the third option, he can cut the middle, the base line, or as shown here. This move is tough on the switching defense. Also shown are shots by 4 and 5. The 1 man checks 3, then 5, and 4 last.

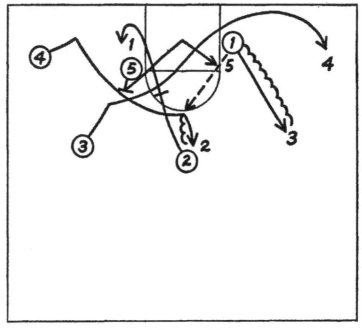

Diagram 64

Now the *rotation* on the fourth option. If a shot is not taken, 1 or 4 will normally have the ball more than 5. They dribble out (5 would pass the ball out) to their new spots and the offense continues. Like the third option, 1 becomes 3, 2 takes the 1 spot, and 3 goes to 4; but 5 will stay at 5, and 4 becomes 2. This type of rotation is a little faster than in the third option because 5 gets to his place quicker. Remember you can keep the good rebounder on the board by putting him in the 5 spot.

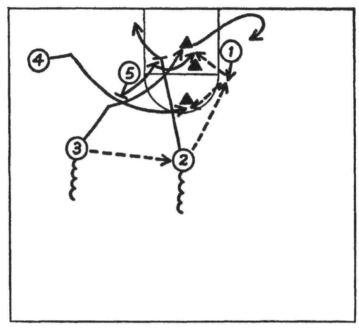

Diagram 65

This is a variation on the way of running the fourth option. After screening for 3, the 5 man turns to the *inside* to form **a** double screen along with 2 to help 4 get his shot. After 4 comes by, 5 slides over 2 looking for the pass, and 2 moves to the board to rebound.

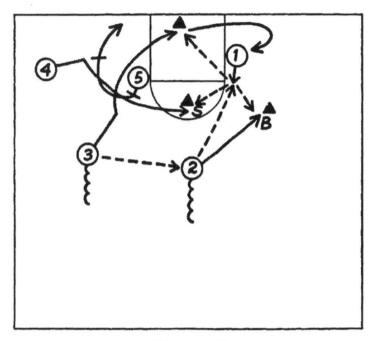

Diagram 66

Here is the way to run the fourth option and *keep the same two good rebounders* on the board. After screening for the 3 man, 5 turns to the *outside* and screens on 4's man. He then goes to the board. 1 checks 3, then 4, and last the 2 man, who delays before moving over. 1 also rebounds along with 3 and 5. For fast break defense, it is best here to let 4 stop the ball and 2 balance.

This method is also worth considering when you have two tall boys who move only fair and are not good outside shooters.

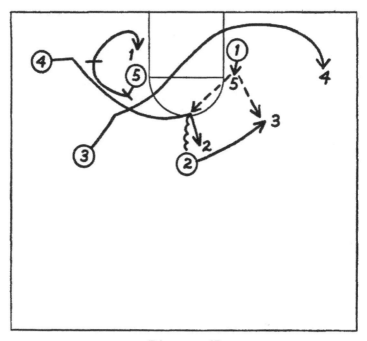

Diagram 67

This is the *rotation* when using the option drawn in Diagram 66. Note that as the overload changes from left to right, 5 becomes the 1 man and 1 takes the 5 spot, and neither has much moving to do. 2 goes to 3, 3 to 4, and 4 takes the 2 spot.

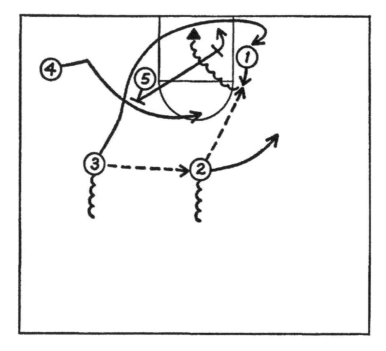

Diagram 68

Here is a good movement that can be used in the type of fourth option shown in Diagram 66. Instead of 5 screening for 4, he moves across to pick for 1, who drives through the middle. Since 3 has already cleared the lane and 4 is going to the circle, 1 has a lot of room in which to drive. 5 rolls off to the basket for good rebounding position and a possible pass-off from 1.

Chapter 8

The Fifth Option

THE INITIAL THOUGHT BEHIND THE DEVELOP-ment of the fifth option was to give the 3 man another method of starting the offense. Originally he would bring the ball up the floor and pass to either 2 or 4. This, in a way, restricted the offensive opportunities by eliminating the chance to use the 5 and 1 men. The logical player to use was 5, as any pass to 1 could be quite dangerous. So by installing this option, the entire offense gained additional flexibility and balance and the defense's problem increased.

Another reason was the opportunity to use the 5 man as a potential scorer at the beginning of the offense. This forces the defense to consider and to defend him, thus taking some of the attention away from the 2, 3, and 4 men. It was thus more difficult for the defense to get set for only the basic parts of the Shuffle—the third and fourth options.

An additional advantage was gained in the ability to move the defensive personnel and, if a shot was not taken, to be able quickly to continue the offense with a different option. When the defense is forced to move, each player must alter his defensive thinking to his required job in the new position. This movement also serves, in some degree, to hide the basic maneuvers of the Shuffle, and this has become an essential part of the success of this offense.

113

The first thing to teach is that the 5 man must expect the pass anytime the ball is in front of him. He is in a fine position to receive the pass, being 15 feet away from the basket and to the side of the circle, so it is not a problem getting the ball to him. Once he has the ball, he is in position to be a good feeder or an effective scorer, and in designing the various fifth options, decide what you want out of this player. Do you want him to basically feed or do you want him to look initially to score?

As in the first option, we have used several variations. These are offered in the following pages with the single purpose of giving you a choice as to which one you may want to use. It is not possible to use more than one without confusion.

Anytime you are developing a pattern when the post man or center has the ball, it is normal to think of the split. This has been a fine offensive idea for years, and especially if the post is used as a feeder. The best way to use a split on the side is to feed the post from the corner or forward position because the moving screen created by the first cutter is very hard on the defensive man on the second cutter (Diagram 69). The tip is for 3 to pass and stand still. The 4 man then knows the fifth option is on and he is to feed the 5 man and cut first. If a shot is not obtained, players are in, or can get to, their new spots quickly and continue the offense. All that has to be done is for 5 to pass out to the 2 or 3 spot.

Diagram 70 offers interesting and profitable opportunities. First, the 3 man has a solo cut to either side of 5, and that move is difficult to defense. Following 3's play, the 1 man moves out to screen for 2's cut on the weak side. The 5 man has three choices: he can feed 2 for the close shot,

1 for the middle distance shot, or make his own play. If 1 gets the pass and does not shoot, he takes the 2 man's job and can quickly continue the offense.

The theory behind Diagram 71 is very simple. The plan is to use 3's cut past 5 as a chance to score in close and also as a fake to hold the defense in place and give 5 the good chance to shoot. Usually 5 will go to the middle with a short dribble and jump shot as 1 and 2 move to new spots to occupy the defensive men on them. The weak point is that 4 does not move. To continue the offense, 5 again only has to pass out to the 3 or 2 spot.

Diagram 72 shows another fifth option possibility that is designed to offset the sinking or sagging defense by getting the shot over from close range. Proper timing should free the 4 man first, with 1 the second choice. If other defensive men are forced to play their assignment and can not drop off to help, the 5 man will have a one-on-one situation to exploit.

Diagram 73 is based on the idea of getting the shot for one particular player and can be used for the *Last shot* situation. The double screen for 4 will give him time to get the shot away, and he also has an excellent chance to drive the middle.

The triple split is illustrated in Diagram 74. Good team speed makes this a very effective option. In addition to the shot possibilities shown, 5 has a very good drive back to the outside. The big center can be used to advantage in this as a feeder and scorer.

Diagram 75 is virtually the opposite in theory to 74. Here the plan is to get the ball to your outstanding player at the 5 spot and let him work a lot on his own. You can clear 1 along the baseline and give 5 all of one side to

work. A skillful player can do a lot with that much room
and you should teach him to turn and face the basket so
he can see the defense.

We have used the option shown in Diagram 71 more than
any other, mainly because we had the player to make it go.
He was Rex Frederick, a 6' 5" boy who could out-run every-
body on the squad. An excellent driver from in close, he
could take care of the ball in close quarters, making successful plays despite the most concentrated defensive
efforts.

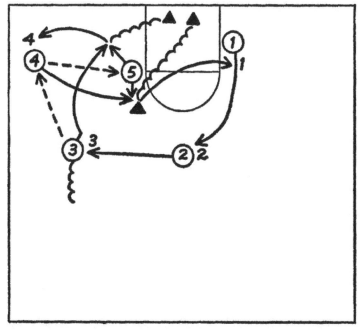

Diagram 69

Here is the ever-popular split, run from the side. The tip is 3 passing to 4 and *staying* in place rather than moving. This alerts 4 to feed 5 and tells 5 to get position for the pass. 4 cuts over the top but is under control to help 3 time his move so that they cross very close to each other. If the defense switches, 4 will be open, if they stay man-to-man, 3 is the best possibility. While 5 is mainly a feeder, he can get a good hook shot to the middle behind the 4 man. 1 and 2 move to occupy the defense. In the rotation, 5 keeps his spot, 1 goes to 2, the 2 man moves to the 3 spot, 3 becomes 4, and 4 takes the 1 spot.

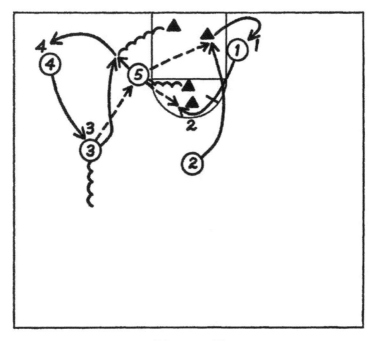

Diagram 70

After 3 feeds 5, he uses a solo cut to either side and goes to the 4 spot if he does not get the ball, 1's screen naturally is slightly delayed because he must move out to help 2, who waits until the screen is set. 2 then becomes the second choice of 5 who may also turn to the middle for his shot. After screening, 1 steps out and has a good outside shot head on the basket. The rotation is shown and the most difficult is 3's move to the 4 spot.

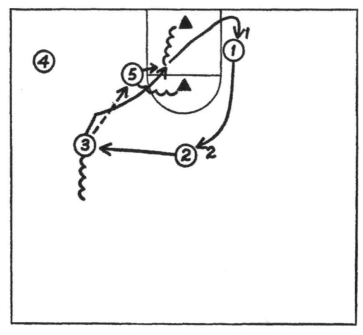

Diagram 71

As mentioned earlier, we particularly like this pattern. 3 passes to 5 and can cut to either side of 5. 3 goes to the 1 spot if he does not get the pass. 5 can pass off or exploit 3's cut to get his shot. The switch here is dangerous and difficult to execute and a strict man-to-man defense will have a hard time stopping both 5 and 3. The pass to 3 can be made as he gets to 5 or can be delayed until 3 is close to the basket. If the early pass is not made, 5 should turn so that he is always able to watch 3 and finishes the turn facing the basket. From this position, he sees the defense better and can pass or shoot more effectively. 4 keeps his place **as** 1 goes to 2 and 2 to the 3 spot.

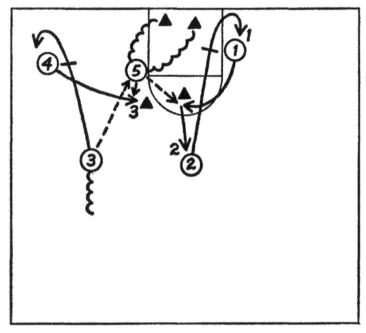

Diagram 72

Here you are first looking for the good middle-distance shot over a
sinking defense. 3 passes to 5 and screens inside for 4, who uses
the screen plus the 5 man to get open. 1 and 2 work slightly later,
and 5 can check 4 and then 1 in that order because the timing is
virtually automatic. 5 will find that he can drive back to either
side as the other defensive men are kept busy by his teammates.

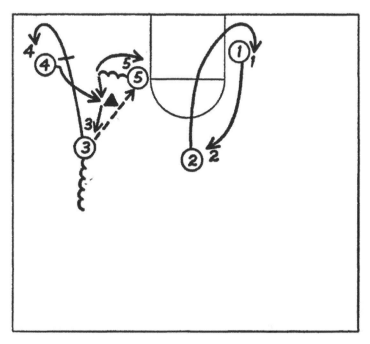

Diagram 73

After passing to 5, the 3 man sets the screen inside for 4. 5 dribbles over to form a double screen to free 4 for the shot over or a drive to the middle. 1 and 2 trade places to keep their defensive men honest. Remember the purpose in this option is to help your best shooter get his shot. Rotation is very simple and the tip, like all of the fifth option variations except Diagram 69, is the pass from 3 to 5.

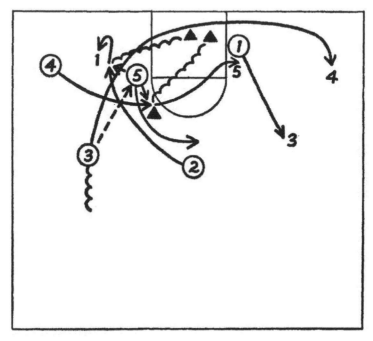

Diagram 74

A word of warning here—good movement and speed is a must and if you have it, try this pattern. 3 hits 5 and cuts through looking for the pass and to continue on to the 4 spot on the *opposite* side. (Note that the overload changes from *left* to *right* in the rotation.) 4 cuts under control behind 3, and 2 follows quickly back of 4. 5 can make a good play by driving back to the outside in behind the 3 man. 1 moves out to the new 3 spot. Any of four men may get the shot and the sequence is natural. Timing of the three cutters is a bit difficult and the fact that 1 is not a potential scorer is a handicap to a slight degree. The rotation is shown as the overload changes. 5 can dribble out to the 2 spot if the shot is not taken.

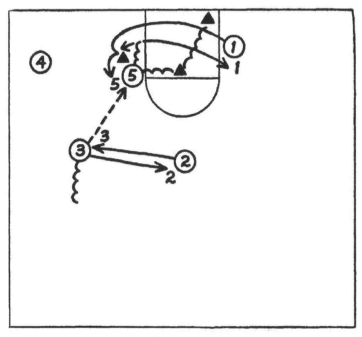

Diagram 75

The plan in this pattern is to give the 5 man as much room as possible in which to get his shot. 3 passes to 5 and changes spots with 2. 4 holds his spot as 1 clears across the baseline. 5 should face the basket after getting the ball, look first for his shot, and next take the ball to 1 for a close jump shot.

Chapter 9

The Turn-Over

THE TERM TURN-OVER REFERS TO THE CON-tinuity of the offense and specifically the use of the third or fourth options after either of these has been run and a shot was not taken. It is not necessary to repeat the same option. As an example, the fourth option can be run, the players rotate in doing this and then come back with the third option. Some coaches call this *two rotations,* but we prefer the term *turn-over.*

You will find that the turn-over makes the offense twice as effective. When quickly executed it is extremely hard to defense. In fact, we believe that we can always get a good shot on the turn-over regardless of what the defense does. The reason is that each defensive man suddenly has a new defensive job and must adjust his thinking to the new problem in a split second. For example, the man at the 3 spot must play the cut off the 5 man and then has to defend against the 4 man. One time he is defending outside and the next moment he is forced to play inside or on a corner man. This is one of the strongest points in favor of the Shuffle.

At this time you may wonder what is the method of getting a first option and then a third option run. We call that a 13 play with the first digit designating the first option to be run and the second digit indicates the next option.

The number 24 would mean a second option followed by a fourth option. This overall method enables you briefly to request for repeated use of the basic Shuffle options, the third and fourth, or a preliminary option followed by one of the basic options. You can also call for a basic and then a preliminary option by using, as an example, the number 31. You would then get a third option and next a first option.

The turn-over has another worthwhile use. It forces players to learn the rotation perfectly or be embarrassed by being out of position. To accomplish this, have the players, during offensive half-court drill, run one turn-over or more before a shot is taken. This makes them move and think until it becomes automatic action. Only then will the players be properly schooled in all the five spots.

The turn-over can also be used as a semi-delay game when it is still too early to stall and another basket or two are needed to make it safe just to hold on to the ball. If you don't get the baskets but have worked the pattern and held on to the ball, you will often find that enough time has been consumed in the turn-over then to go into the delay or stall game with reasonable security. We have had this happen on several occasions.

The quickness of the turn-over is largely dependent upon the players going to the 1, 2, and 3 spots. Since the 2 man rotates to the 1 spot, he goes to that spot and will break to the board if he sees a shot taken. Either 4 or 5 will rotate to the 2 spot and, if they get the ball there, will dribble quickly to get exact position, giving the other players a brief moment to get to their spots. The 1 man takes the new 3 spot and dribbles out a couple of bounces or simply moves to the spot if he does not have the ball.

In Diagram 76-A, the third option is run, but the 1 man does not pass to 3, 4, or 5. He takes the ball out with a dribble to the 3 spot, which is his normal rotation. This is the simplest and most common way to start the turn-over. In Diagram 76-B, the fourth option is run with 4 taking the shot in the circle. The fact that a third option was followed by a fourth illustrates that a turn-over is not restricted to a repetition of the initial opinion and actually any option may be used. An example is Diagram 77-A and 77-B, where a third option is first and then repeated.

The next illustration, Diagram 78-A and 78-B also repeats the third option with the main purpose of showing how to execute the turn-over when 4 gets the pass. If he cannot shoot, 4 passes out to 5, who will move to the 2 spot or to 1, who takes the 3 spot. On the turn-over, 3 gets the shot on a base-line cut.

Another often-used method of setting up the turn-over is shown in Diagram 79. On the third option, 5 gets the pass from 1 and, instead of shooting, takes a short dribble back to the 2 spot. He then passes to the 1 spot and on a fourth option, and the new 5 man gets the shot.

In the preceding diagrams, the third option has been run first. Now we will start with the fourth option. In Diagram 80-A, 1 passes to 3, who dribbles out instead of shooting. He passes back out to 1, who has moved to the 3 spot. Then, as shown in Diagram 80-B, the fourth option is repeated with 4 shooting after the screen by 2.

In Diagram 81-A, 5 receives the pass and cannot shoot, so he dribbles toward the 5 spot on the other side of the lane and passes out to the 3 spot (1 has rotated to 3). In 81-B, the fourth option is repeated with 3 shooting after cutting through the middle off 5's screen.

The next two diagrams start with the fourth option, and in the turn-over the third option is executed. In Diagram 82-B, the 5 man takes the shot. In 83-B, 4 is the shooter as he breaks across into the lane.

The last three diagrams in this chapter illustrate the use of what is often called a preliminary option followed by a basic option—the third or fourth. We call this a play series to avoid confusion with the turn-over. Diagram 84-A shows the first option (previously used in Diagram 28) followed by a third option, which composes a 13 play.

A 24 play is the basis for Diagram 85—a second option (Diagram 42) followed by the fourth. In Diagram 86, a 53 play is shown. This is a combination of the second option (first used in Diagram 71) and a third option.

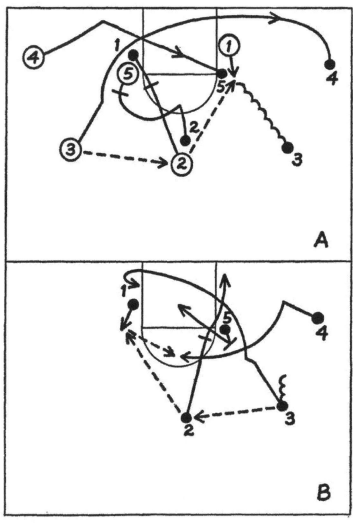

Diagram 76

In *A,* 3 passes to 2 to start the third option. The 1 man keeps the ball and dribbles out to become the 3 man. Other players complete the rotation. The turn-over begins as 3 passes to 2, 2 to 1, and 1 feeds 4 on the fourth option. Remember that 5 determines whether the third or fourth option is run when the ball is moved 3to2to 1.

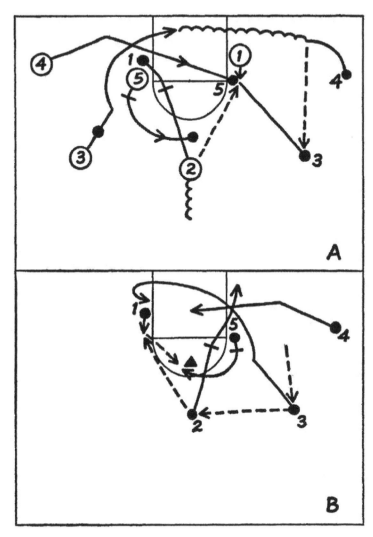

Diagram 77

At the top, 2 brings the ball up, passes to 1, and the third option is run. 1 feeds 3, who cannot shoot and dribbles out to pass to the 3 spot. Note that 1 has moved to 3 in the rotation to receive this pass. In *B,* the third option is repeated with 5 shooting in the circle on a pass from 1.

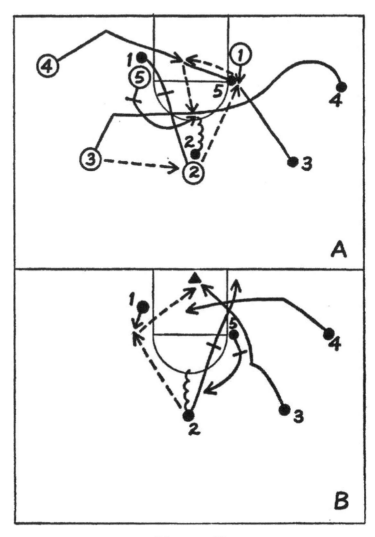

Diagram 78

In A above, the third option is run. 4 gets the pass from 1, does not shoot, and then passes out to 5, who dribbles to the 2 spot. Since only one pass is needed now (2 to 1) to start the turnover, the rotation must be completed quickly. The turn-over in B is a repeat of the third option as 3 shoots after a base-line cut

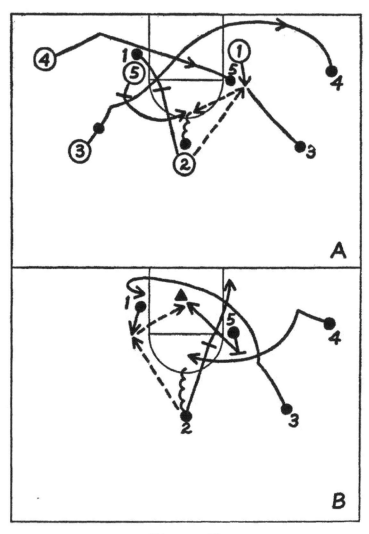

Diagram 79

The top diagram shows a third option with 5 passing up the shot and setting up the turn-over by dribbling quickly to the 2 spot. In *B,* the fourth option is used in the turn-over and 1 passes to 5 sliding back for the shot. 5 should make this move when he is bumped as he screens for 3 or he will be delayed too long to use the third option effectively. The main effect is the delay of the 4 man, who must wait to react on the move by 5.

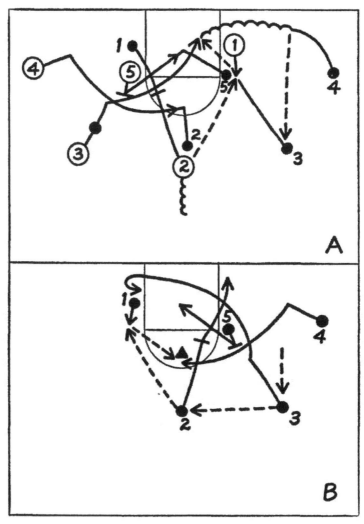

Diagram 80

The fourth option is shown in A above. 3 keeps the ball, dribbling clear to pass out to the new 3 spot. With the rotation completed in B, 3 passes to 2 to start the turnover which is another fourth option. The finish is l's pass to 4 as he comes over 2's screen for the shot. This screen by 2 will actually occur farther to the right than can be clearly shown in the diagram. 2 will, in court conditions, move almost over 5's original position.

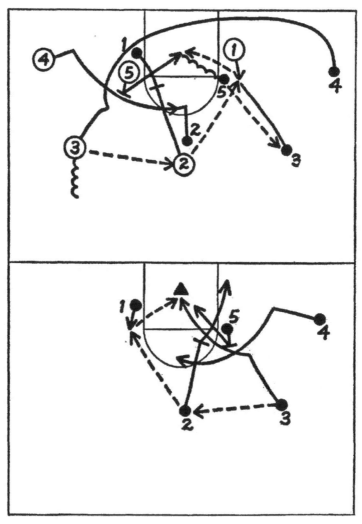

Diagram 81 (A and B)

In *A,* the fourth option is illustrated. 5 gets the pass from 1, does not try to shoot, but dribbles across to the new 5 spot to pass out to the 3 spot. At the bottom, the same option is used in the turnover, and 3 shoots after his cut through the middle. You can run any number of turn-overs retaining possession until you get the shot you want. Naturally, good, sharp ball handling is a must.

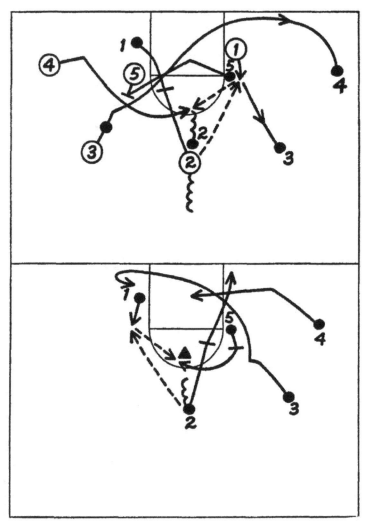

Diagram 82 (A and B)

A is a fourth option with 4 starting the turnover by going to the 2 spot with ball after a pass from 1. A quick rotation is necessary in this situation because the pass (in B) from 2 to 1 starts the third option. Here 5 receives the pass and shoots the middle-distance shot in the circle. You will find that the rotation and resulting turn-over are quicker when the fourth option is used first, especially if the ball is at the 2 spot.

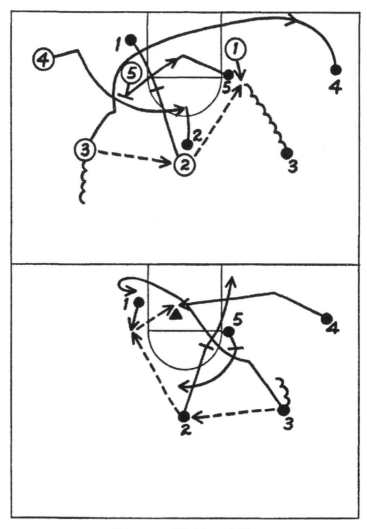

Diagram 83 (A and B)

The fourth option is shown in A, with 1 passing up the cutters and dribbling to the 3 spot. In *B,* a third option completes the turn-over and 4 shoots from in front of the basket. The 1 man looks for 3, 4, and then 5, plus being at liberty to take the shot himself.

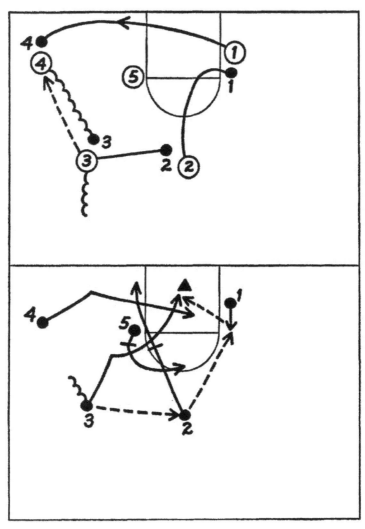

Diagram 84 (A and B)

This is our first diagram of the play series—the *13* play. The diagram in A shows a first option previously drawn in Diagram 28. 3 passes to 4 and goes away from his pass. 4 checks 1, then 5, and can also drive the middle to shoot or take the ball out to the 3 spot and begin another option. In J5, with the ball at 3, the third option is run and 3 shoots after cutting by 5's screen.

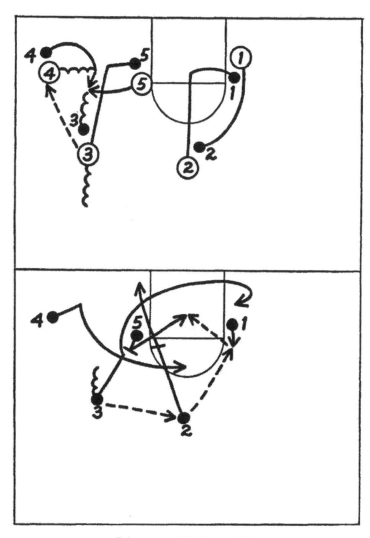

Diagram 85 (A and B)

This is a *24* play. The second option is run in A, as 3 passes to 4 and moves inside to help set the double screen. As 4 dribbles in, 5 rolls out to get the hand-off and then passes up the shot to dribble out to 3. Rotation of other players as shown. The fourth option is run in *B*. 5 gets the pass from 1 and the shot. 5 should use this move a lot against a switching defense.

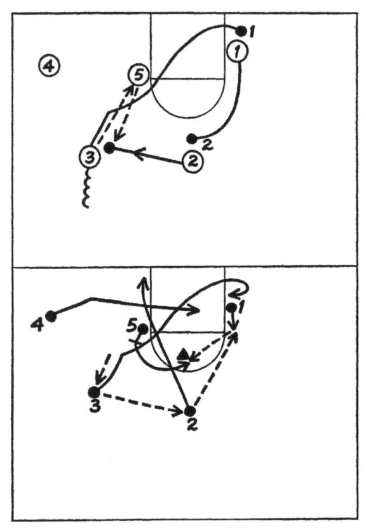

Diagram 86 (A and B)

Here you have a *53* play—a fifth option followed by a third option. In *A,* a simple fifth option variation is used giving quick rotation plus good scoring chances for 3 and 5. Here 5 passes out to the 3 spot, and in *B,* the 5 man shoots in the circle on a third option.

Chapter 10

Free Lance Play in the Shuffle

LIKE ALL SET PATTERN OFFENSES THE SHUF-fle can be defended by a good ball club that is well drilled in sound defensive play. So to get the maximum out of this offense, free lance play not only must be permitted but must be systematically planned, players taught when and where to go on their own and then encouraged to do so. Then when you can combine pattern play with intelligent free lance moves, you have a good offense.

After teaching the set options, we have spent more and more practice time on free lance play and have similar diagrams to the ones in this chapter in each player's play book. In charting game films, we have found that Auburn teams have been able to balance their scoring between fast break, free lance, and pattern scoring. You can do the same with your team by putting virtually equal emphasis on all phases of offensive basketball. Regardless of when, how, or where a team gets the ball, it should quickly be a threat to score because that is the only way to keep continual pressure on the opponent's defense. In our opinion, Kentucky teams are the very best at this. We always warn our players that they will never get a chance to relax against the Wildcats. We like and use this rallying cry: "Keep taking the ball to them—keep going at them!" There is no question that such an attitude fosters aggressive play, the way good athletes want to play. They want to compete, to challenge the opposition, and you can't do that by walking around.

In this chapter, you will find free lance moves to use from each spot, grouped for each position. Diagrams 87 through 90 illustrate plays that the 1 man can make. He handles the ball and is relatively close to the basket where a short move can give an excellent shot. Take Diagram 87 first and you will see 1 driving back to the outside. He should do this anytime the defensive man (note the X) is still tight on the inside when he catches the ball. The 1 man does not worry about 3 cutting into him as it is 3's job to avoid this. If 1 does not get all the way in, he will at least get a short jump shot on the baseline. A good time to use this move is when 2 brings the ball up, as 3 is slightly later cutting through.

In Diagram 88, 1 drives the middle *behind* 3 and before the 4 man gets into the lane. This can be used when the defense is in normal position on 1. You will find that boys who are strong and tough in close will make effective use of this idea. Our fine All-Conference boy, Rex Frederick, was very effective with this because he had the tools to make the play. Encourage the boys who have special talents to use them.

Diagram 89 is set up by 1, who actually helps 3 to get the shot. When 1 cannot feed 3 in the normal area, he can slide dribble back to the outside and let 3 hook around him for the short jump shot or even a drive into the middle. This is especially effective when the 3 man is well defensed on his normal cut.

You should incorporate the shot shown in Diagram 90 into shooting practice. The defense often considers 1 just a feeder and will not pressure him too much. When this is the case, put good jump shooters in the 1 spot and tell them to look for 3 first and next their own shot. Never pass up the 3 man if you can get the ball to him. You can work very hard moving the ball and screening and still not get a better shot than 1 has from his position.

Now we go to the free lance plays available to the 2 man, as illustrated in Diagrams 91 through 94. In Diagram 91, you see 2 breaking over 1 to shoot there or to drive closer for the shorter shot. He can also dribble and use 1 as a screen. These moves are always left to the 2 man's judgment. If he does not get the pass from 1 or if he gets the ball and has to pass out without getting a shot, 2 continues in his normal rotation to the new 1 spot. If 2 shoots over 1, he takes the job of stopping the ball in the fast break while 1 goes to the board.

The normal passing lanes for teams using the Shuffle is often 3 to 2 to 1. When the opponent starts to overplay toward the short side of the overload (toward the 1 and 2 spots), it is necessary to offset this overshifting of the defense by taking the ball back to the overloaded side. How to do this is shown in Diagrams 92 through 94, and is initiated by the 2 man. He may get the shot himself by the move shown in Diagram 92. He can use this regardless of whether the third or fourth option is run. In Diagram 93, he sets up the 5 man; in 94, he does the same for the 4 man.

Diagram 95 shows the three paths that 3 can use for his cut. With this much freedom, 3 can free lance and take advantage of his defensive man's position. Jimmy Lee, one of our co-captains in 1959, was an expert at this. He had played in the Shuffle in high school under Coach "Bubba" Ball at Baker High in Columbus, Georgia and he was well coached before he came to us. Jimmy could start his cut from the 3 spot and then peel-out over the 1 man so quickly that his man never knew where he was going. He could also shoot very accurately and very quickly on this move and was always one-two among our leading scorers.

The 4 man has good free lance opportunities when 3 passes to him and follows the pass or goes away from the ball. Diagram 96 demonstrates what 4 is at liberty to do. He can shoot from the side, drive the middle using 3 and 5 as helping screens, or quickly hit the base line. The third and fourth options also give him good chances to score, so he is no longer the neglected man in the Shuffle Offense.

Diagram 97 shows the two moves that 5 can use in the third and fourth option plus a new move recently added to the offense. This is the quick break (he does *not* screen for 3 on this) over the 1 man for a jump shot there or a close shot on the base line. This maneuver is a bit more effective if run when 2 brings the ball up because 5 has more time to cut in front of 3. No harm is done, however, if he cuts behind 3 and in front or behind the 2 man. It is basically a part of the third option and does not create any confusion.

Diagram 98 illustrates optional moves by 5 in the third option and though it is not shown in a diagram, 4 has the same moves in the fourth option. The 5 man will get the ball a lot in or at the edge of the circle. If his defensive man is so close that the shot then is difficult, 5 can drive to either side for the better jump shot.

To conclude the chapter, let me repeat that more baskets are scored by free lance play than from set patterns. So give the players freedom—and let *them* play the game. You help by intelligent planning and careful teaching of the best way for them to play.

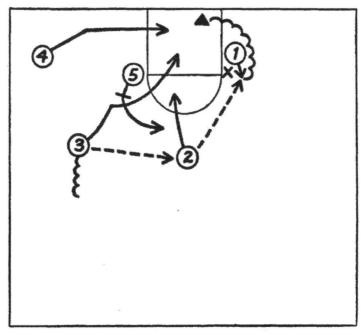

Diagram 87

When 1 has a defensive man on him who is overeager and tight to the inside, he should, upon catching the pass from 2, *drive quickly back to his outside.* He may get in for the lay-up, but if he does not, he has a very close jump shot near the board. It is best to use this when 2 brings the ball up, as 3 does not cut as quickly and there is less chance of his affecting the play.

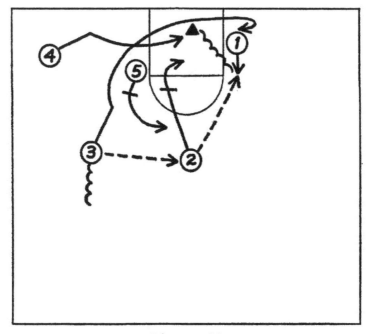

Diagram 88

Here 1 *drives to the middle* in behind 3 though he is not trying to use 3 as a screen. This should be used by the players who are effective with the dribble in close—they are usually the stronger and more aggressive players on the team. 1 should exploit this move against normal or close defensive play from the rear and must move quickly before 4 comes across.

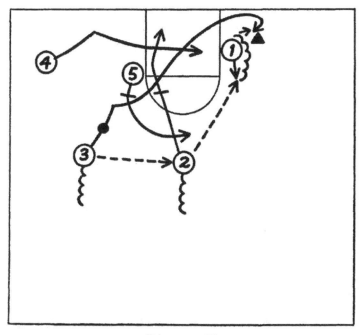

Diagram 89

This maneuver is used by 1 to help 3 get the shot when good defensive play will not let 3 have the ball while he is in the lane. 1 uses a slide or shuffle dribble to get position for 3 to come around him. This cuts off the defensive man, permitting 3 to shoot a close jump or to drive the middle if his man comes around the screen.

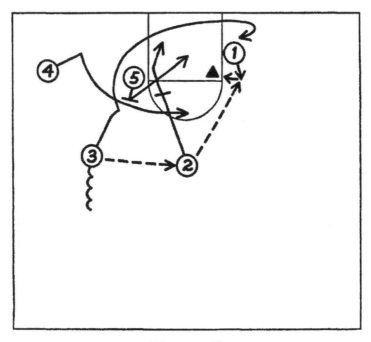

Diagram 90

This is a *very* good play for the good jump shooters to use when in the 1 spot, especially if the defensive man is shorter or playing loosely. 1 should always check 3 first because that is the chance for the lay-up. When 1 executes his pivot to the inside, he finishes facing the basket in perfect position to shoot. By taking this shot, he forces the defense to respect him in this spot and eases the pressure on his passing to 3.

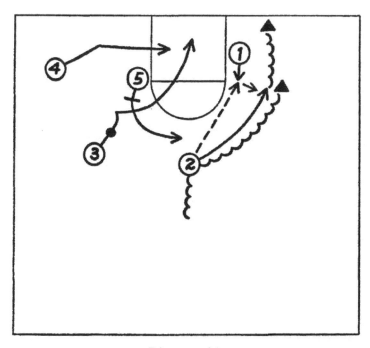

Diagram 91

Here is one way to use the 2 man more as a shooter and to keep the defense honest. 2 can follow his pass to 1 for a jump shot over or a drive to the base line for a closer shot. He can also dribble over 1 for the same shots when he brings the ball up or when 3 does and passes to him. 2 continues to the new 1 spot in the normal rotation if a shot is not taken.

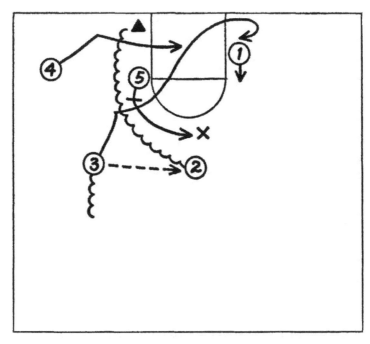

Diagram 92

Here is a way to reverse the pattern when the defense overplays toward the short side of the overload on 3's pass to 2. This is a third option. 2 drives to the *outside* of 5 and *behind* 4 cutting across the middle. 2 has a good chance to go all the way and can also stop anywhere along his path for a jump shot.

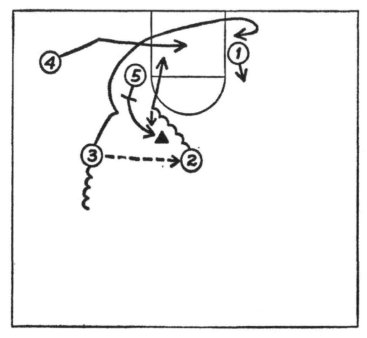

Diagram 93

Again 2 reverses the offense as 5 moves in the third option. This time 2's dribble is to the *inside* of 5 and he hands off, screens, and goes to the board if 5 shoots. If a shot is not taken, 2 goes to the 1 spot—his normal rotation.

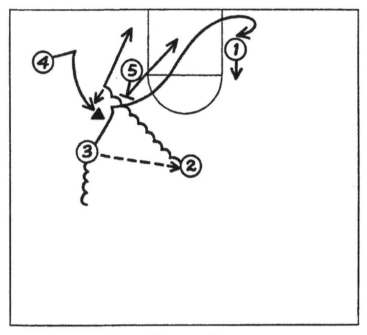

Diagram 94

This is similar to 93 except a fourth option has been initiated by 5 and 2 hands off to 4. When 2 starts his dribble to the inside, he does not at first know whether he will pass off to 5 or 4, but he does know that one of them will be moving in a path leading to and over him. Rotation is not changed.

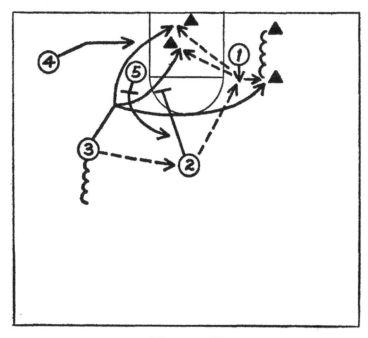

Diagram 95

The moves by 3 are shown here to illustrate that his choice of three paths to cut on constitutes free lance play. By using his choices, 3 can take advantage of his defensive regardless of how he plays. In addition, Diagram 89 shows another opportunity for 3 to score.

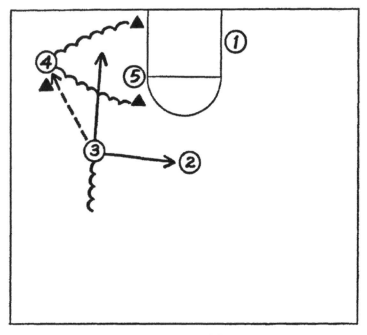

Diagram 96

Here you have the plays that 4 can make after receiving the pass from 3. He can shoot from the side, drive across the middle for a shot over 5, or hit the baseline with a quick dribble before 3 gets to him. 4 also has his moves in the third and fourth options to give him scoring chances.

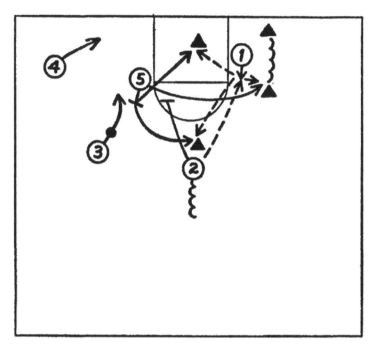

Diagram 97

In this diagram, the maneuvers available to 5 in the third and fourth options are shown. The break over the 1 man is relatively new and is used as a part of the third option. It is useful when the defense is consistently switching on the 3 and 5 men, and is somewhat easier to use when 2 brings the ball up.

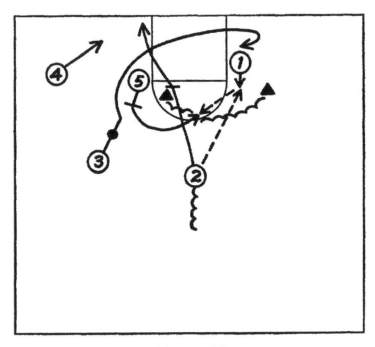

Diagram 98

The idea here is to show that 5 has the right to move in order to shoot when he goes to the 2 spot and is defensed too tightly to shoot from this spot. As shown here, he can drive *right* over 1 or back to his *left* where he does not have a screen but does have ample room in which to get his shot. In the fourth option, 4 has the same free lance movements at his disposal.

Chapter 11

Using the Post Man With the Shuffle

ONE OF THE WEAK POINTS IN THE SHUFFLE as it was first used was the inability to use the talents of the big post man. The third option pulled him away from the basket and critics and opposing coaches did not overlook this fact. Then we devised our conception of the fourth option to get the big man on the offensive board more often and also gave him the privilege of going to the board when he was at the 1 spot. However, these variations will not give the really fine post man enough opportunity to do the job for his team that he is capable of doing. Since it is vital to get everything useful out of every player and to exploit their strong points to the maximum, some additional option must be devised to utilize the big center who plays best at the post with his back to the basket.

The team pattern shown in Diagram 99 is our basic theory of how to incorporate the skills of the big man into the Shuffle Offense. It is a first option variation (often called *circle)* and the signal is 3's pass to 4 *with the post man at the 5 spot.* This is a double signal, but it can be used with the normal amount of drill as our experience has proven. We had particular success with this when Bill Mc-Griff was our center because he could score off the post and, in addition, was an excellent outside shot. It should

155

be explained here that if Bill was at the 5 spot but the 3 man did not want to use this option, he would pass to 2 and start the third option. Since all players play all the spots, you can easily regulate the number of times you use the post man in this manner.

To further explain Diagram 99,1 cuts along the base line and 4's first choice is to feed him as close to the basket as possible. If this pass is not open, 1 continues his cut to take 4's place as 4 dribbles out and across looking to feed 5 as he moves. Right here you can use the big man. If the defense is playing *in front* of the post man, you can pass *high over* the defensive man and there is no one to sink off the weak side of the defense in time to help because 1 has cleared his defensive man out of the way and 2's man cannot sink in time. Should the defensive man play to the base line side, 5 can drive back through the lane and he is almost unstoppable. With the defense to the inside, 5 can drive the baseline and if the defensive man is behind, 5 has all the plays available to a post man plus the advantage of the open area vacated by 1's defensive man.

It is not always possible for 4 to feed 5, so additional plans must be made and put into effect if the big man is to be used properly. When we were faced with this problem, we incorporated our old Post Offense into the Shuffle. These ideas are illustrated in the next three diagrams.

Diagram 100 shows what is called a *Post Cut*. When 4 cannot pass to 5, he passes to 3 who has moved over just past the middle of the floor. The 5 man moves with the ball using footwork just like the defensive man, keeping his back to the basket and not crossing his legs. He is always expecting the pass and 3 feeds him if he can. If 3 can not make this pass, he moves the ball to 2. The 5 man has continued his move across the lane and takes a post position facing 2, who also looks to feed him.

Diagram 101 is what is called a *Post Reverse.* Note that 5 moves with the pass from 4 to 3. If the ball is passed back to 4, then 5 reverses his direction to take the pass from 4. This movement is one reason for the sliding steps by 5 and enables him to change his direction quickly. He is also able to take advantage of the defensive man who tries to lead him into position and stay in front to deny him the ball.

Diagram 102 is called *Post over* and may well be the most effective of this series. The 5 man sets this up and it gives him a chance to act on his own. He initiates this pattern by moving to the weak side *when 4 catches the pass from 3.* Upon seeing that 5 has moved across the lane, 4 passes quickly to 3 and 3 feeds 5 or hurries his pass to 2. Now 2 has the chance to hit the post man. The advantage here is that 5 can *choose his position* by moving early and can take a spot close to the board if he so desires. If the ball is moved fast, the defensive man will have great difficulty getting a position in front of 5. And when the defense is forced to play behind a good post man who is close to the basket, the offense definitely has the upper hand.

Diagram 103 illustrates a different team pattern to assist the use of the post man. The main idea is to give 4 the chance to feed 5 without being hampered by a dribble. At the same time, 1 pulls his man away from the basket to give room for the pass over to 5, and 2 takes 3's place as he moves to the weak side. It is wise to keep your corner men out as far as the foul line to give 5 more room to operate and to make it harder for the defense to sink out of the corners.

Now let us go into the general theory of how to feed and use a post man. It is necessary for the passer to *see the position of the defensive man* guarding the post and then aim his pass to the open side. There are *four sides* to the post man—the front, rear, left, and right—and the defense cannot play in four places at once. So you can get the ball to him by intelligent passing.

The accepted theory of proper defense on the post is to keep the ball away by playing in front. This idea can be hurt by clearing out behind the post (Diagram 99) and passing high and over to him. On this pass, it is best to keep the pass on the *strong side* of the basket as it is easier to handle and is more difficult for other defensive men to get to. Start the pass *from above the head* to avoid the very slow type that is in the air too long.

It is always wise *to clear for the post man* in order to give him room to operate. You can clear behind him or the corner in front of him and thus create a one-on-one situation. The good center cannot be defended when you give him this advantage.

If you are depending on the post to carry a big scoring load, it is best to keep cutters away from him. Other players should pass and move, but in paths that do not bring extra defensive personnel into the area of operation of the post. It is also smart to feed the post man when he is moving because a stationary man can be hampered more by good defensive action.

If you have gotten the ball into the post man once, you can get it back to him if he passes out. It is an excellent plan to hit him first. If he does not want the shot then, he can pass out, improve his position, and get the return pass in a more advantageous spot.

One very grave danger to any coach is having too much offense. If you have the good big man and plan to use the Shuffle, limit the number of options. I would recommend options one (Diagram 99), three, and four, plus normal free lance play. If another option is added, use one of the simpler second option variations. As you continue to use this offense and your players learn it better, then consider more additions.

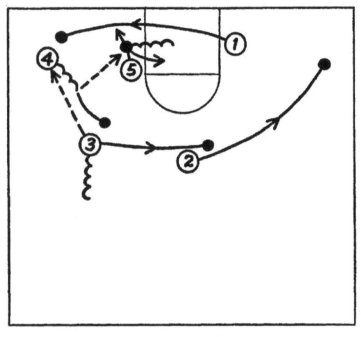

Diagram 99

Commonly called *circle,* the tip is 3's pass to 4 plus the post man being in the 5 spot. 4 should use 1 some by passing to him close to the board. Note that 1 has cleared the weak side corner and 2 is swinging wide to stop even with the foul line extended. 5 can improve his position by moving down the side of the lane. 4 feeds off his controlled dribble. If the defense is in front of 5, the pass should be high and over in line with the strong side of the basket. 5's best play is the drive back through the lane ending with a close hook shot.

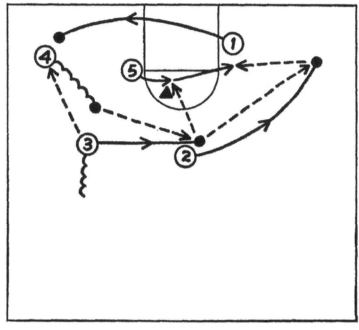

Diagram 100

This is the *Post cut,* signaled by 4 passing to 2. 5 slides with the ball and is fed by 3 or 2. Sometimes when 2 makes the pass, 5 can drive in close for the shot.

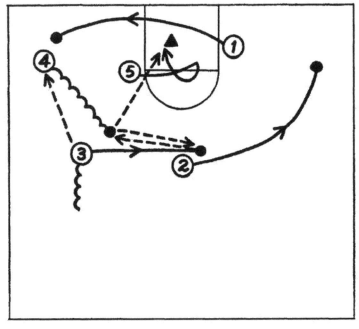

Diagram 101

Now the *Post reverse* which is first a cut and then a reverse. 5 moves with 4's pass to 3. As the ball is passed back to 4, 5 reverses to get the feed from 4. This move will often give 5 a driving lay-up when his defensive is tending to overplay toward the ball and has gotten too far toward the weak side.

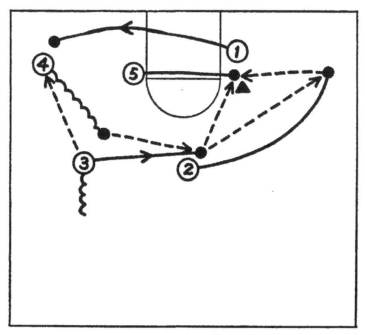

Diagram 102

The *Post over* is very effective for the good hook shot. 5 sets this up by moving to the far side of the lane as 4 gets the pass from 3. He selects a spot relatively close to the board, yet still out far enough to use the board on his shot. The ball is moved fast to 3, who will feed or pass quickly to 2.

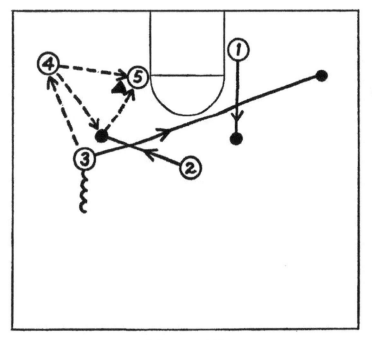

Diagram 103

This team movement pattern can be used to aid the post man and also as a free lance pattern. 4 is able to concentrate more on getting the ball to the post, while other players move to maneuver their defense men and thus cut down on the defensive sink. 1 comes out quickly, 3 moves behind him. 2 moves over to take 4's pass in case the ball is not fed immediately to the post.

Chapter 12

Practice Drills for the Shuffle

YOU MAY ALREADY HAVE THIS QUESTION about the Shuffle: "How can players be taught to play all five positions?" This is the normal reaction, and we have faced the question many times. It can be taught virtually as fast as any other offense and one reason is that it stimulates and challenges the player to learn and he reacts well to this situation.

The initial step is to teach the numbers and exact location of the spots. First give the players copies of the options you plan to run—do this before your practice begins. For the first week, make regular lesson-type assignments for each day. As an example: Monday—first option; Tuesday-second option; Wednesday—third option. Continue until you have covered the complete offense. Be sure to give the assignments to the players for the entire week, not just day to day, so they can study a lot before the practice sessions.

It is extra work to devise tests, but such time is well spent. You can mimeograph blank forms and at a squad meeting have each player diagram any or all of the options. Set a time limit on the test based on how long the players have used this system. Another good idea is to send individuals to the blackboard to diagram and explain in detail the option assigned him. We use this more than the written test and find it very successful. If the players are slow to learn, have them study for 15 minutes before the workout.

We believe strongly in using drills that are a part of our style of play and are always searching to expand these drills. *Coaching is basically teaching* and one major problem is time. You continually race the clock. Since there is never enough time, you must search for the best drills to teach the most skills to the largest number of players in the shortest length of time. Too often, drills are run because the coach has used them before; not enough thought and planning is put into getting the best teaching job done. You cannot expect a player to do something in a game that you have not had him do numerous times in practice.

As you first start to teach an option on the court, go to the blackboard and draw and explain each man's play. Then take one team and have them trot through the option. Next have each boy go to another spot, repeat the option, and change spots again. After each of the five players has worked at each spot, ask for questions. When these have been answered, split the squad into two units for the drill. I would recommend the controlled pace until the players have a reasonable idea of what to do. Do not expect them to be perfect—accept the early mistakes, correct them, and keep working. If a mistake is made but possession of the ball is maintained, you are never in much trouble.

The drill shown in Diagram 104 is a lay-up drill based on the third option. We use this six minutes a day during shooting practice and work three minutes on the left and then three on the right. Let either 3 or 2 bring the ball up and *insist* that they start at mid-court to get the timing of the pattern. The rotation is different to the third option but players learn it without difficulty. You eliminate the 4 man and 3 drops out after his shot and a new player A comes in to the 1 spot. The advantages here are the added number of times the players get to run the option plus the fact that they shoot the lay-up as they get it in a game. The drill is called third option lay-up drill.

It is wise to free lance this drill at times. Only a few of the free lance plays are shown to avoid congestion in Diagram 105. To get this run, all you have to do is tell the players to free lance the drill.

To expand the drill, first add a passive defensive man on 3 and tell him to play to either side early or straight back. That will give the 3 man very valuable work in seeing his defensive man (Diagram 106) and making the proper cut. To avoid contact and possible injury, have the defensive man play under control and stop when he hits the screen. Also you should have the 5 man catch him with his hands instead of the body. Note in the diagram that the defense is playing to the inside so 3's cut is to the baseline or outside.

The next step in developing the drill is to add a defensive man on the 1 man (Diagram 107) along with another on 3. To provide recognition, let these defensive men hang a colored scrimmage shirt around their neck. Do not have them put the shirts on as it takes too much time getting them off. Let these defensive men keep their jobs for four shots and then change them.

The defense on 1 is also passive and merely heckles the passer, but by being there will force concentration by the 1 man. You can also make this small segment a scrimmage condition—but not on the 3 man because of possible injury.

Also in the shooting practice while working on outside

shooting, we use a drill called third option outside shot. This is a simple two-man drill and is shown in Diagram 109. You start with 1 having the ball. Then 5 steps out to simulate his screen, rolls out to get the pass from 1, and takes the shot. The 1 man rebounds the shot and takes the 5 spot and the drill is repeated. Be sure to have the drill run from each side to give the players practice shooting after moving right and left. Also insist that the 5 man be very exact in his movements and when he rolls out, do it quickly and be set to shoot fast when he catches the ball. It is also worthwhile to expand this drill by adding the 2 man to 1 and 5, plus using a passive defensive man on 5. To get the normal effect, tell the defensive man to play loose on 5 as many teams do to help on the 3 man when he cuts. Now you have a game situation for the 2 man and he will actually have a defensive man to screen. You will find that players must learn to *find the man to screen* or otherwise they will not be doing a good job.

In Diagram 111, you have offensive men 1, 2, and 4 with the defensive man on 4. Here you are giving the 2 man more experience in screening, as in Diagram 110, but the 4 man is doing the shooting. This ties in with the fourth option as the preceding diagram does with the third.

Diagram 112 shows the drill we use with a full ball club. The squad is split to use both baskets and to give more work for each player. It is sound thinking to aim at developing seven or eight players who will do the bulk of the playing and you should keep these together as much as possible. If some players are about equal, use half of them with the first team for part of the drill and then switch them. This will give them a chance to be prepared and accustomed to working with each other along with assisting in developing good morale on the squad.

The average length for this drill should be 10 to 15 minutes. The rotation is not affected, but after a shot is made the players move to different spots in numerical order—1 to 2, 2 to 3, and so forth. The 5 man drops out and A comes in at the 1 spot. This insures each player of practice in each spot and enables the extra players to get their turn.

All parts of the offense are run and it is also easy to designate any particular options you may want to drill on more than others. It is the best way to work on the turn-over, and to do this simply say "Turn-over before a shot is taken." You should do this often to assist the players to learn the rotation and then to form the habits that enable them to use the offense effectively. You will develop good ball handling and movement through this turn-over practice and will realize how easily the continuity of the offense can be maintained. Always insist that the ball go in the basket before the offense is stopped. This drill, more than any other, teaches the Shuffle offense.

We do not like to scrimmage half court and do very little of it. Instead we will use a skeleton scrimmage with a couple of defensive men as shown in Diagram 113. Put the defensive men at the positions needing the work most, and with fewer players on the court you can see more and do a better coaching job.

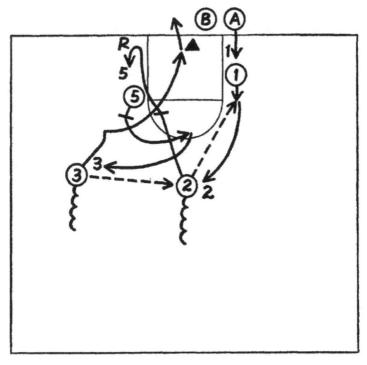

Diagram 104

This is called the third option lay-up drill. A 4 man is not used. Use half of the allotted time on an overload left and the other half on an overload right. The players rotate from 1to2to5to 3. The shooter (3 man) drops out and A comes in at the 1 spot. Vary the method of bringing the ball up (let 2 and 3 do it) and have the ball start at mid-court. 2 always rebounds the shot and passes out to the 3 spot.

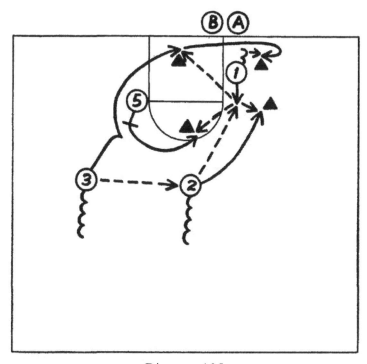

Diagram 105

This drill has the same rotation as shown in Diagram 104, but players are told to run their free lance plays. As shown here, 1 dribbles back for 3 to come over him, 2 cuts over 1 instead of moving in to screen, and 5 rolls out even though he does not get a screen. Virtually any of the free lance moves can be used, and this is an excellent way to teach them.

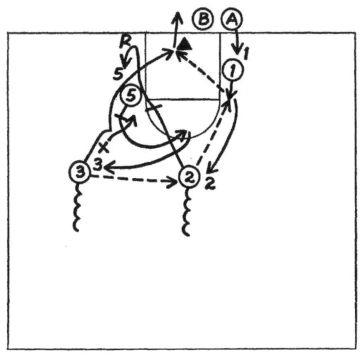

Diagram 106

To teach the 3 man to see the defense better and use 5's screen, a defensive man is put at the 3 spot. He deliberately plays to the inside (as in this diagram), forcing 3 to make the correct cut to the outside or base line. He will also play to the outside or drop straight back so that 3 faces all the possible defensive situations. The defensive is passive and merely for drill purposes. After all the other players have gone through the drill at each spot, change the defensive man.

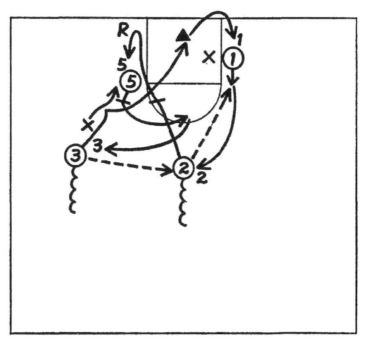

Diagram 107

Here the third option lay-up drill is expanded by adding another defensive man put on the 1 man. This gives better practice for the players when they work in the 1 spot. They have to consider that defensive man on their pass to 3 cutting and this gives them additional work in a game condition. This can be the scoring pass and must be delivered at the right time and position so that the 3 man can handle it and shoot without difficulty.

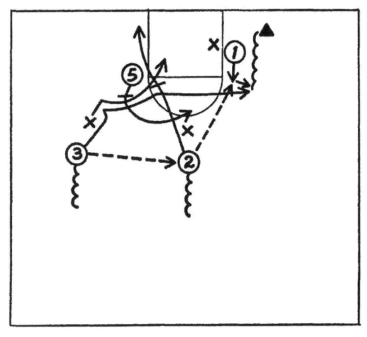

Diagram 108

Now another defensive man is added. He works on the 2 man, but not at full speed. He, like the others on defense, is permitted to overplay to either side occasionally to encourage the 2 man to react to the free lance play when it is available. Here the defensive man on 3 has played the screen very well, and 3, seeing this, adjusts his cut to go over the 1 man and get the shot.

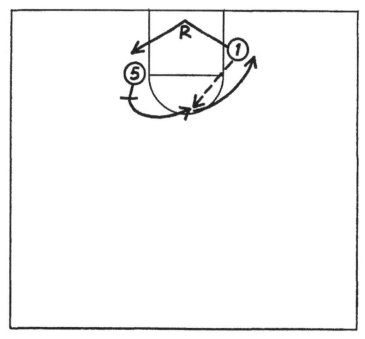

Diagram 109

This is called the third option outside shot and is one shot that you can get anytime you want it. 5 steps out to set his screen, hesitates, and then rolls out to get the pass from 1. 5 shoots a set or jump shot and 1 retrieves the ball. Then the players change jobs and keep repeating the drill. This will force players to practice on a definite move and shot where they get it in the game.

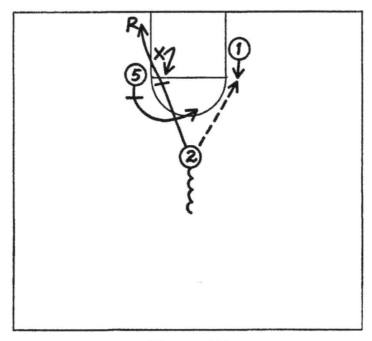

Diagram 110

Here a defensive man is included to work on the 5 man and a 2 man is added to the offensive unit. This gives better timing work, aids the 2 man in learning how to screen, and helps the 5 man to time and use the screen by 2. In addition, 2 gets good offensive rebounding work. Have players merely rotate from 1 to 2 to 5. Be sure to have them work from each side and let the defensive man trade jobs with an offensive man after all players have shot.

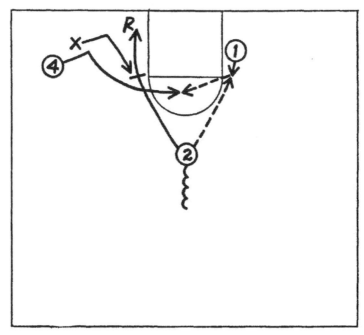

Diagram 111

This drill has the same purpose as Diagram 110, except that the shooter works from the 4 spot. Remember that the 2 man hesitates one count after passing to 1 before moving in to screen. The defensive man should sink quickly to the inside as the ball goes to 1 because many defenses do this and 2 has to set his screen as he will in a game. He must find the defensive man and screen in his path.

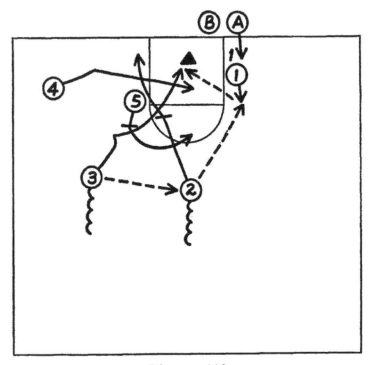

Diagram 112

This is the best drill to use when a full team is working. Players change spots after the ball goes in the basket and A comes in at the 1 spot, 1 goes to 2, 2 goes to 3, 3to4,4 to 5, and 5 drops out. When you need extra work on a particular option or the turnover, all you need do is stop the drill and tell the players what you want done. Let 3 or 2 bring the ball up and insist that *all phases* of the offense be used until you want to specialize. Too often players will repeat the same option unless told to do otherwise.

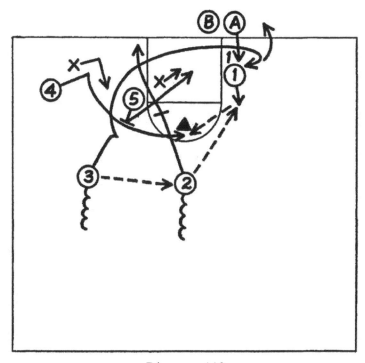

Diagram 113

The purpose of this diagram is to show that one, two, or three defensive men can be added to closer approximate game conditions. Have the defensive men play passively at times, and at others make it a scrimmage condition. Use the same system of changing spots after a shot is made as in the preceding diagram.

Chapter 13

The Fast Break With the Shuffle

IT IS DOUBTFUL THAT ANY OFFENSIVE SYSTEM is easier to combine with the fast break than the Shuffle. If a shot is not taken or a missed shot has been rebounded by the breaking team, players simply have to fill the nearest spots to begin the offense. In this situation, the ball determines the overloaded side and, since it will normally be outside, players will not have difficulty seeing the ball and reacting to that side.

The fast break has always been a controversial issue, some teams refusing to use it in any form. Since we feel that the breaking game should be a strong part of the offensive plan, let us look at its advantages.

1. *It gives the opportunity for the easy basket.* To fight through a set defense every time down the floor is a very tough job and the fast break basket can have a demoraliz ing effect on a defense. While some may ridicule the style of play, the basket still counts the same two points and it only takes one to win a ball game.

2. *A team can get more shots.* To score, you have to shoot the ball and, when the break is properly run, the re sulting shot is usually the high percentage shot. On the nights the shooting percentage is down, you must rely on defense and getting more shots if you hope to win.

3. *It keeps pressure on the defense.* When a team must

hurry to defense when it gives up the ball, eventually the defense won't get there in time. Too, there is not time to rest—no breathing spell if the opponent is always bringing the ball at the defense. The slightest mistake can result in a basket and the pressure builds to great heights on the defense.

4. *The fast break promotes aggressive play.* Every player likes to shoot and score and the running game gives them that chance and gives it often. The battle is carried quickly to the defense and forced upon them whether they are ready or not. The fast break team *attacks* with all possible speed and power and that is certainly aggressive basketball.

5. *It offers a better chance to overcome a lead.* If your team is behind, you need to shoot the ball and score to get back in the game. Often you cannot afford to use 30 sec onds or more to get the shot. You cannot use the time nec essary to work the ball around looking for the good shot when time is running out. The only hope is to score quickly and get the ball back as soon as possible.

6. *More interesting for players and spectators.* I've never known a player who did not like to fast break and the spec tators feel the same way—unless you boot the ball and fail to get a shot when you really need one. Athletes are trained to play and to compete and they like to do it without con suming a lot of time.

 It is not only proper but also wise to consider both sides of any issue. The fast break may cause some added floor mistakes but it is not a certainty that it will. It is admittedly more tiring and demands additional substitutions, but players are supposed to be in top condition and to be able to play a long time with a minimum of rest. Teams may try to force the break when they don't have it but this can be corrected by good coaching. That is what we get paid to do—to coach. So we definitely stand on the side of the fast break and recommend most serious consideration of this part of the offense.

When do you have a true fast break? Only when the offense *outnumbers the defense* or *can beat them to the basket—even* with one man providing he has the ball. These are two simple rules to control the fast break and to tell players when to go ahead on the break or when to slow up and run the set offense. Many teams will shoot when even with the defense—two-on-two or three-on-three. This is a sound theory when a good percentage shot is taken and the shooter is under control. After all, you may have to work hard against a set defense to get the same shot, and you have as much rebound power at the board as the opposition.

How do you get a fast break? You get it initially by *anticipating the opportunity* or seeing that your team is going to get the ball and getting that one or two step jump. Next you have to *get the ball out* and then get *three men* in the front wave and in the three lanes. After that it is good ball handling combined with speed that delivers the fast break basket. Actually speed is not a dominant factor. Many teams can run but do not have outstanding speed. They simply get started in a hurry.

When do the fast break opportunities come? The best or most productive chance is *from the interception*—there is absolutely no planned defense for the break in this situation. The only hope is very quick reaction by the players that will offer some kind of defense. The *loose ball* is next in rank followed closely by the *long rebound.* We are very partial to the long rebound because more of these are available. Next, the *short rebound* is not too productive against a well-organized team but will hurt the team that is weak on defensive balance. The *free throw made or missed* is another chance and so is the *jump ball*. In addition, you should always look for the opportunity when you get the ball *out of bounds* in the back court. A long pass can give the easy basket if the defense is not alert.

At best, the fast break is a fluid thing because any player may be in it and in any spot. The fast break drills, therefore, are used for mainly one *reason—develop* the *habit* of trying to get the break. When this habit is formed, simple rules will be sufficient to govern the organization of the running game. Here is a set of such rules.

1. To get the ball out, look to pass first and next to dribble. (This dribble must be *up the floor—not* to the side.)

2. Get a middle man. If you do not see one, take the ball to the middle. When a player takes the middle, he calls it out to let others know.

3. Flank men stay wide until they reach the foul line. Then they head for the basket.

4. Use the middle man, especially from mid-court to the basket. He can dribble in this area and force the de fense to declare itself.

5. If the middleman is jammed, take the ball up the side. The flankers close in to create a two-on-one situation which is even better than three-on-two.

6. The middle man stops at the foul line *unless* he can take the ball to the basket for the shot.

7. The flankers do not arrive at the basket at the same time. One should be ahead of the other.

8. Flankers never cross under the basket.

9. Be very careful of passes between the flankers. Use the middle man.

10. The front wave of three are the rebounders.

11. The last two players down the floor are trailers. They furnish defensive balance and do not penetrate past the top of the circle. Use them for shots over the defense that bunches under the basket.

The 3 lane fast break drill as shown in Diagram 114 is very good to get the running, ball handling, and to start developing the fast break fundamentals. Insist that the ball be moved fast and the players use all their speed. A few mistakes at this time will not hurt you. This is a good way to teach the middle man to stop at the free throw line unless he can drive all the way. Also the flankers get excellent work on staying wide and not getting to the basket at the same time. They should be staggered and the late man is often the best bet for the shot. In our conference, the University of Tennessee is an outstanding example of how to use this man—and they always have a fine running game.

After the fundamentals are learned, it is wise always to work against some type of defensive play. In Diagram 115, X-1 and X-2 are used to fight the 3 lane break. These defensive men play normal fast break defense with X-2 taking the side the ball goes to and X-1 dropping back deep to play the pass across. X-1 is responsible for forcing 1 to pass and will not let him drive to the basket. The defense is also permitted to free lance, and X-1 may take 1 early and force him to pass off. Then the flankers should close in to cut off X-1 and create a two-on-one situation. These two drills are also very good at the end of practice to develop stamina as the players get a lot of running in a short period of time. Each threesome has a ball and the drill is repeated as soon as all the groups have assembled at the other end of the court. We often have a group go back and run the break again when a mistake is made. This forces concentration and attention to good ball handling.

Next comes team fast break work and Diagram 116 shows one way of running the break from the defensive board. The coach has the ball and takes the shot. All players simulate screening out their opponent and then react to rebound. The *outside* man on the *strong side* gets the outlet pass and the *outside* man on the *weak side* takes the middle. The *weak side* corner man moves to be the other flanker. The last two men down the floor are trailers and do not go past the top of the circle. Be sure that the players let one of the trailers shoot after first taking a lay-up. Thus *two* shots are taken and the trailers become a definite part of the break.

In Diagram 117, the *middle* man was the *weak side corner* man and the two *outside* defensive men fan-out to be the flankers. As 3 opens up to get the outlet pass, he should be facing the *inside* of the court with his back to the side line because he can see more of the floor in this position. We believe that this break gets started faster than any other and we use it when our tall boys are fast enough and are good ball handlers.

Since the pass interception, loose ball, and long rebound are the most successful opportunities to fast break, you should get drill time on these situations. In Diagram 118, the coach throws the ball on the floor to simulate the loose ball and he may also deliberately pass to a player or bank a shot hard off the board to get a long rebound. In these situations, a set pattern is not feasible and players react from habit to form the break. The player who takes the middle must always yell out to let others know and thus avoid confusion. If a middle man has not shown, the man with the ball should dribble to the middle and call out, "I've got the middle!"

Diagram 119 shows how to get opposition that is so very necessary in perfecting the running game. X-3, X-4, and X-5 are initially on offense and one of them is permitted to shoot. Then a scrimmage situation develops in the battle for the rebound, to get the ball out and to form the fast break. When the break is under way, X-l and X-2 are in position to play the defense against it. This is a very worthwhile drill and will really test the overall effectiveness of the fast break attack.

We think that the fast break should also be used from the free throw whether the shot is made or missed. Diagram 120 shows it from a missed shot, and from this position it is very easy to form the break. The 1 man is always the middle man, 2 and 3 the flankers, and 4 and 5 are always the trailers.

The next three diagrams show the fast break when the free throw is made. It is basically a four-lane break with 3 and 2 coming up the floor together *unless* one can get in the break faster, in which case only three lanes are used. The illustration in Diagram 121 demonstrates the use of the long pass to a flanker who drives for his shot. The 1 and 4 men always cut hard to the *opposite* corners from where they are lined up on the foul lane, and 5 is the late trailer.

Diagrams 122 and 123 show two free lance plays that are used when the defense will not let you have the fast break lay-up. The 1 man sets this by breaking in to set a post near the foul line extended. This fast break plan puts con tinual pressure on the opposition as well as giving several opportunities to free lance quickly against a hastily formed defense.

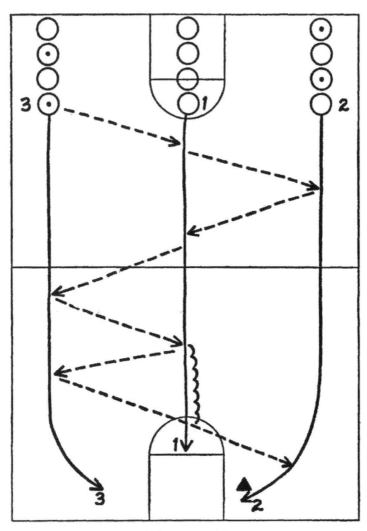

Diagram 114

Squad is divided into groups of three and each group has a ball. Start with the ball at the side assuming that the outlet pass has been made. Here 3 passes to 1 as the first group starts the drill. Move the ball by fast passing until past mid-court. Then the middle man can dribble. Demand top speed, accurate passes, and that the shot be made. Here 1 stops at the foul line as he should and feeds 2 for the shot. Note that 2 reached the basket ahead of 3, who is the late man. Next group starts on coach's whistle. Drill continues until all groups have worked, and then is repeated from the other end of the floor. Have players work in the middle and the flanks.

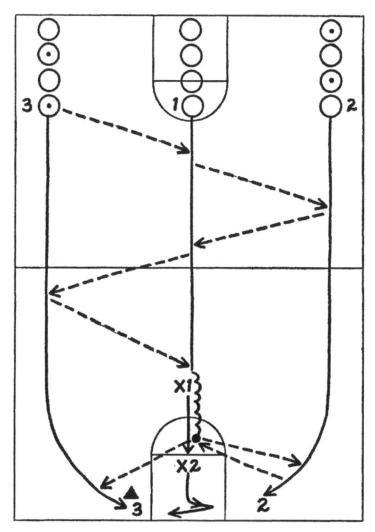

Diagram 115

Defensive men have been added in X-1 and X-2. X-1 works on the middle man to slow him down and make him pass to the side. X-2 protects the basket and plays the side the ball is passed to as X-1 sinks deep. Here 1 passes to 2, who returns the pass instead of shooting. This is the reason for having 1 stop at the foul line—the flankers know this and will use him if they cannot shoot. 1 then feeds 3 for the shot. A pass from 3 to 2 is risky and should be used only when certain of its completion. It is safer to use the middle man.

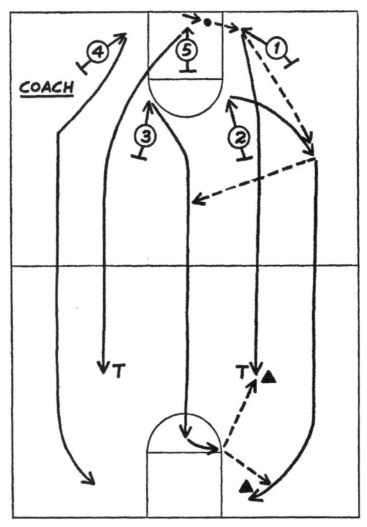

Diagram 116

This is a team fast break drill. The squad is divided into teams and the centers get a ball for their team. As the coach shoots, all players first screen out imaginary opponents and then turn and move to get rebound position. 1, 4, and 5 take the short rebounds while 2 and 3 are responsible for the long ones. As 1 rebounds (this establishes the *strong* side), 2 (strong side and outside) rolls out to take the outlet pass, 3 takes the middle and calls out "I've got the middle." 4 (weakside and inside) becomes the other flanker. 1 and 5 are the trailers and, in this case, 1 gets the second shot after 2 shoots the lay-up. (Other passes are not shown to avoid congestion.) After each team has run through this, then repeat from other end of court.

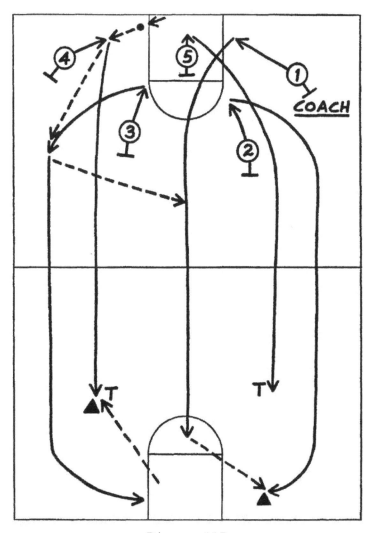

Diagram 117

This fast break is different from 116 in that the middle man, number 1, comes off the base line as 3 and 2 both open up and take the flanks. If you have inside players who can run and pass, this is the faster pattern. If you prefer to have your smaller players handle the middle in the break, Diagram 116 will get them there most of the time. This is another coaching decision and should be based on your players' talents.

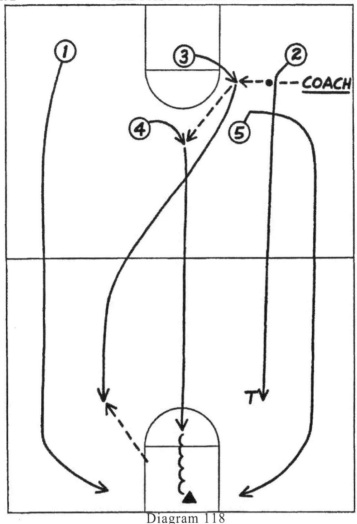

Diagram 118

This diagram demonstrates a fast break after sudden possession of a loose ball. The coach rolls the ball on the floor (he can also lay it down, pass it close to a player for an interception, or take a shot). Here 3 recovers the loose ball and should call "Go!" to alert his teammates. The outlet pass in this case is made to 4 taking the middle. This pass should be made to the strong side or to the middle. (Avoid the cross-court pass to the weak side.) Getting the lanes filled is based entirely on reaction and habit as no organized pattern can be run in this situation. Note that players have changed positions. After each fast break, have players take a different spot. They must be able to fast break from any spot as the opponent's offense may force them to play defense in any area on the court.

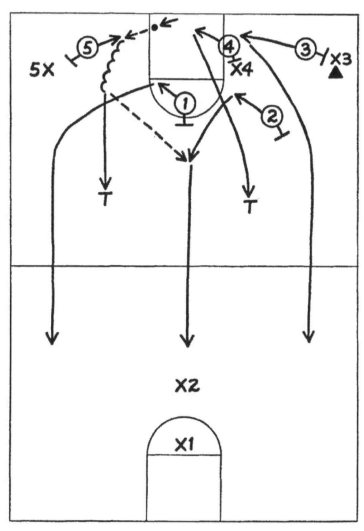

Diagram 119

Once the fast break pattern has been learned, it should almost always be run against opposition. Here X-3, X-4, and X-5 are offensive men and they are permitted to shoot. After the shot, they hit the board for the rebound and a scrimmage situation exists. X-1 and X-2 are stationed at the other end of the court to defense the fast break. This drill demands strong rebounding and a good outlet pass or dribble to get the break started. Note that 5 recovered the rebound, started up the floor with a dribble and then passed.

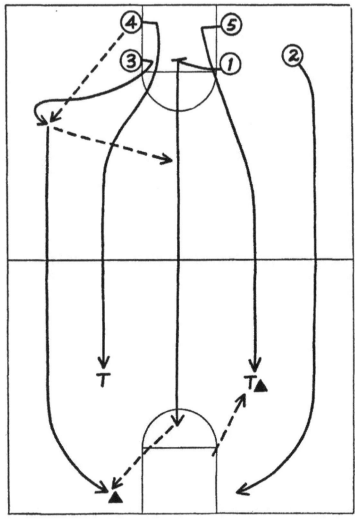

Diagram 120

This shows the fast break after a missed free throw. The ball can be tipped out to 2, but a pass is the only way on the other side. 1 screens the shooter (assisted by 3) and hits the middle. 3 and 2 are always the flankers and 4 and 5 the trailers. Always let one of the trailers shoot.

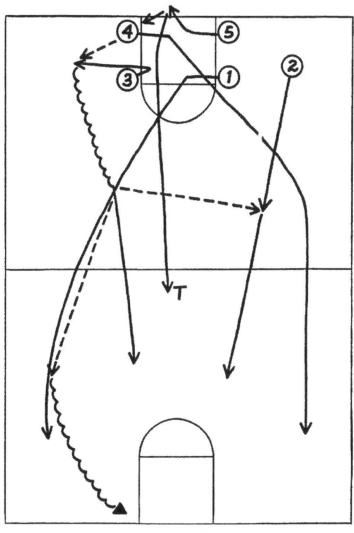

Diagram 121

Here is the fast break pattern from a free throw that is made. 5 quickly takes the ball out and passes to 3 (2 delays his break so that 5 has *two* men to pass to instead of one), who starts up court with a fast dribble. 2 slants toward the middle as 4 and 1 break for opposite sides. In this situation 3 passes long to 1, who goes in for the lay-up. Basically, this is a four-lane break, though 3 could take the middle if the defense was quickly outnumbered, making it a conventional three-lane break. 5 is a delayed trailer and available for defense at the basket should the opposing team recover the ball and fast break right back.

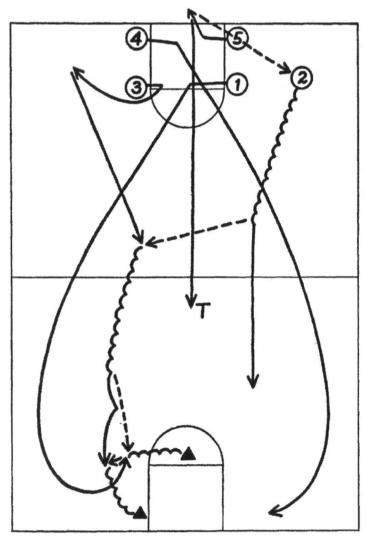

Diagram 122

This diagram shows a free throw (made) fast break where the opponent gets back fast and will not give up the close-in shot. In this situation, 1 breaks back to set a post, 3 passes to him and cuts by to *either* side. 1 can pass off to 3 for the drive, turn and shoot, or dribble to the middle for a shot. 2 assists 5 as a trailer to give defensive balance while 3, 1, and 4 hit the board.

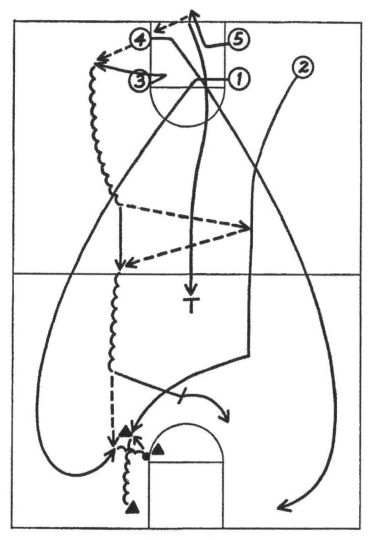

Diagram 123

Here is another free lance play at the end of the free throw fast break that has been stalled by good defense. It is fundamentally a *second guard around* play. 3 passes to 1 and goes opposite to screen for 2. The 1 man dribbles in to give 2 a better cut and has the option of passing off to 2, turning in place to shoot, or dribbling to the middle for the shot. 3 and 5 are the trailers as other players rebound. Any three-man play can be run in this situation.

Chapter 14

Planning the Practice Sessions

ORGANIZATION AND PLANNING, THE BIGGEST problem facing the young coach as he starts his career, must be rated at least 50 per cent of the coaching job. As a player, he was concerned mainly with what he had to do, with no conception of the time his coach was spending on practice plans, scout reports, charts, trip details, and so forth. This chapter is written as a help in planning your practice sessions.

One of the first things to do is to make a checklist of *things to be done* and break this list into four sections.

1. *Before Practice Starts*

   Include such things as ordering equipment; checking eligibility; checking lights, score board, and dressing rooms; arranging physical exams; giving flu shots; preparing player notebooks, travel plans, expense estimate, and scouting schedule.

2. *In Practice*

   Work on man-to-man offense, zone offense, offense against man-to-man press and zone press, delay game, out-of-bounds plays, fast break, jump balls, fundamental drills, defensive drills for individuals and groups, and team defenses (man-to-man, zone, press).

198

3. *Before First Game*

Check the timers and scorers, make up pass lists, get eligibility blanks signed, recheck the clock, and have charts made.

4. *After Season*

Select letter winners, elect captain, order awards, make final check of charts, check for new records, and conduct inventory of equipment.

These are not all the things on our checklist, and yours will also have items that are not listed. The above are used to explain what is meant by a checklist and how one may be organized.

I ask your indulgence in the following material as I refer to what we do. It is the best way I know to explain our procedure and the wording is not intended to be boastful.

Our practice begins October 15. Players are alerted when they return to school to start running, exercising, and working with weights so that they are in fair condition for the start of practice. They are especially urged to run out of doors and gradually to build up their stamina by distance running. Flu shots, plus the physical exams, are given to all players, managers, and coaches.

During the first week of organized practice, almost all the work is out of doors and consists of exercises, running (that is gradually increased), volley ball, weight work, and shooting practice. In the second week, workouts are limited to one hour and 15 minutes a day and consist of shooting drills, light fundamental work, offensive drills on the options (prior lesson assignments for each day are made), and fast break drills for conditioning. Weight training continues and is held three times a week. This is limited to the toe lifts.

What is the purpose of the first two weeks of work? First, it is a conditioning period and it is not a rigorous program because good physical condition cannot be rushed. It is a gradual process and must be handled accordingly. We have found that we simply do not have any real foot problem and will not have a half-dozen blisters in a whole season. This can largely be attributed to outside running, the short sessions on the court, and good shoes. We also expect players to have a good understanding of the offense and to be able to go through a two-hour-plus practice by November 1 without excessive fatigue.

Now the real workouts begin. Extensively planned practice schedules are made. We always make three copies of the practice schedule so each coach and the manager has one. The manager must keep accurate time on each drill and alerts the coach *one minute before* each drill is to end. The two hour practice schedule is divided as follows:

> 30 minutes—Shooting practice
> 10 minutes—Free throws
> 40 minutes—Offense
> 40 minutes—Defense

The combined 40 minutes of shooting work never varies —this is an absolute must. The remainder of the allotted practice time is divided 50-50 between defense and offense. This division is iron-clad. Scrimmage time is considered as half defense and half offense and is included in the following schedule:

> 30 minutes—Shooting schedule
> 10 minutes—Free throws
> 25 minutes—Defense

25 minutes—Offense
30 minutes—Scrimmage

Another checklist idea is used to guarantee that enough time is used on each phase of the offense, the defense, and the shooting. Here it is:

1. Shooting (40minutes)

   (a) Lay-ups (b) Jump Shot (c) Outside Shot (d) Post Shots (e) The Drive (f) Tip-ins (g) Free Throws (h) Free Time

2. Offense (40minutes)

   (a) First Option (b) Second Option (c) Third Option (d) Fourth Option (e) Fifth Option (f) Free Lance (g) Turnover (h) Play Series (i) Fast Break from Defense (j) Fast Break from Free Throw (k) Zone Offense (1) Offense Against Press (m) Delay Game (n) Situation Work

   Fast Break .... 10 minutes
   Zone Offense .... 10 minutes
   Set Offense (man-to-man) 10minutes
   Press Offense..................................... 10 minutes

(Allotted time is adjusted when scrimmage is held or when weaknesses require more time.)

3. Defense (40imnutes)

   (a) Footwork (b) Sliding (c) Switching (d) Post (e) Team man-to-man Normal (f) Team Switching (g) Zone (h) Press-Zone (i) Press—man-to-man (j) Fast Break Defense (k) Foul Line Defense (1) Jump Ball (m) Situation work (n) Opponents' Offense

   Individual .... 10 minutes
   Zone .... 10 minutes
   Normal man-to-man .... 10 minutes
   Press *or* Fast Break Defense.............. 10 minutes

Until January 1, and when games do not cause adjustments, practices are two hours or more and usually more.

All drills, whether offensive or defensive, start with the teaching of individual technique and are expanded to units of two or three players and then to team drills. These drills are merely portions of the overall team play. Individual work on particular weaknesses is done after practice ends. We scrimmage more each year and these are for a half game or full game. This procedure will be discussed later in this chapter.

Mid-season practices (January 1 to February 10) are cut to one hour and a half, with a complete day off given to the first team whenever possible during the latter part of this period. The reserves get more scrimmage than the regulars—they always scrimmage on the rest days given the starters. Most of the defensive time is spent on the next opponent's offense and the offensive time devoted to new options or maneuvers plus work against the next team's defenses.

Late season workouts (February 10 to March 1) are normally held to an hour or even 45 minutes. The main consideration is to have the ball club rested and eager to play even though it may not be as sharp. Especially try to have them *mentally* rested and any idea, no matter how strange, can be used. For example, we have recordings played on the speaker system during shooting practice and players supply the records of their choice. A day off here is also in order for the entire squad.

How are our scrimmage sessions conducted? In the very early workouts and during mid-season, we hold these scrimmages for only a half (20 minutes by the game clock) of a game. The time is split into segments—eight minutes using man-to-man offense and defense, six minutes zone, and six minutes press. Eight players compose the first unit and the remainder play with the blue team (or reserves). We do a minimum of scrimmage against the freshmen.

When team conditioning permits, we start full game scrimmages and like to have two a week. One of these will be filmed, and this is very, very useful for coaches and players. In *all* scrimmages, the game clock is run and the managers keep charts that are totaled and available by the time the players have showered and dressed. All scrimmages other than practice games are what we call *situation scrimmages*. The clock is set with a certain time left to play, and the score is also adjusted to give every type of game situation. To us, this is the most worthwhile practice time we spend. Players not only like the idea, but also work even harder because of the keen competition that develops. Here is an example of a typical half scrimmage:

8 minutes: first team —6 points (man-to-man defense—possession first team).

6 minutes: tie score (zone defense—possession reserves).

3 minutes: first team +3 points (press by reserves—jump ball).

3 minutes: first team —4 points (press by varsity—possession reserves).

These periods are adjustable and additional time may be used to work with or against a particular defense that is causing difficulty. By using the game clock and the situation scrimmage plan, teams can be drilled in virtually every game situation and should not often be disturbed by tactical changes in the opposing team's style of play.

We have also given considerable study to the shooting practice part of the workout and have become convinced that *organized shooting* work will pay good dividends. Here is a typical shooting practice schedule.

Free time   .... 5 minutes
Lay-up shooting .... 6 minutes
Jump shot drill ....12 minutes
Outside shooting and post shooting........... 7 minutes

Some adjustment is necessary on the days we work on tip-ins and drive plays. Here is such a schedule:

Free time .... 5 minutes
Lay-up shooting .... 6 minutes
Jump shot drill .... 6 minutes
Drive play .... 4 minutes
Outside shooting and post shooting .... 5 minutes
Tip-ins   .... 4 minutes

The reason behind this type of shooting workout is to insure that players work on *all* their shots and that they spend the *proper amount of time* on each one. Also when you know what type shot a player is going to take, you can do a better job checking his shot motion and suggesting changes when needed. The free time is necessary to help the players loosen up and to work on special shots. It also helps to relieve the restriction imposed on them by the organized shooting.

As for the foul shooting practice, we use *five minutes* of the allotted time in normal drill, but *always after working on the fast break.* Then the element of fatigue is involved and this also resembles to some degree a game situation. Not more than three players work together, each limited to three attempts when on the foul line. The group rotates to the right on the whistle to avoid a stagnant situation and also to get work at different goals. The remaining *five minutes* are split into two periods with a period at the end of each of the first two situation scrimmage segments. These are *one and one* sessions—the player must make the first shot in order to get a second. He never shoots more than two shots. The *one and one* is also always in effect in the situation scrimmage, so as to put the players under pressure as often as possible.

Before closing this chapter, I want to stress again the great importance of very careful and detailed planning for each practice session. The ideas you have just read come from more than 20 years of basketball coaching. Remember that you continually race the clock, that you will never have enough time to do all you would like to do. So plan to use *every precious* minute on the things that are important to your team's success.

While the game of basketball becomes more complex each season, you will be wise always to remember the four *basic essentials of the game:*

1. Get the ball.
2. Move the ball.
3. Shoot a good percentage.
4. Play good defense.

Summary

Let us now assume that you have decided to use the Shuffle or some part of it and briefly discuss the steps to take in developing and teaching the system.

First, *carefully evaluate your personnel.* If you have a good big man, I would recommend the third and fourth options plus options to make the best use of this player. For the team without a tall man, install a first, third, and fourth option, and later add a second and fifth when your team is ready for them.

Next, *mimeograph the options to be used* and put these into playbooks for your players. Insist that they study, and supplement study with carefully planned squad meetings for your explanations and tests of player's knowledge. Be sure that you have first thoroughly studied and mastered every detail of the offense.

Stress the importance of *learning the members* and *exact location of the spots.* This is the first coaching problem. Then *teach the complete option,* not just the several parts.

After the initial learning stage, *work on the turn-over* because this more than any other drill will develop automatic movement. It will also disclose any need for extra instruction for particular players. Pay *close attention to small details*—perfect these and the offense will fall into place.

Avoid the rigid pattern by teaching and encouraging

free lance plays. And *don't neglect the fast break.* The Shuffle fits superbly with the running game.

Finally, sell your players on *team basketball* and the Shuffle as your idea of playing as a unit with a single purpose— *win the ball game.*

Index